Euripides: Bacchae

DUCKWORTH COMPANIONS
TO GREEK AND ROMAN TRAGEDY

Euripides: Bacchae

Sophie Mills

Duckworth

First published in 2006 by
Gerald Duckworth & Co. Ltd.
90-93 Cowcross Street, London EC1M 6BF
Tel: 020 7490 7300
Fax: 020 7490 0080
inquiries@duckworth-publishers.co.uk
www.ducknet.co.uk

A catalogue record for this book is available
from the British Library

ISBN 0 7156 3430 5

Typeset by e-type, Liverpool
Printed and bound in Great Britain by
Biddles Ltd, King's Lynn, Norfolk

Contents

1

Euripides and the Greek Theatre

Euripides was born in Athens somewhere between 485 and 480 BCE, and his life-span coincides almost exactly with the growth and relatively swift decline of his city's power in the Greek world. In his infancy, the Greeks were struggling to avoid the clutches of their imperially-minded eastern neighbour Persia. Victory against all odds at the sea battle of Salamis in 480 – one tradition puts Euripides' birth on the very day of the battle – and the next year on land, sent the eastern aggressors home, but relationships between the city-states of Greece were never the same again. Made newly confident by the major role they had played in securing Greek freedom, the Athenians led an alliance of Greek states against their former enemy, but as the alliance turned into an empire organised for its leaders' benefit, gratitude towards the Athenians for their original services became bitter resentment. The resulting Peloponnesian War, which divided most of Greece between partisans of Athens and of Sparta, began in 431 BCE when Euripides was about 50 and was waged, on and off, until Athens' defeat by Sparta in 404. Euripides died abroad in 406, so did not live to see his city's defeat.

Athens' imperial power made the city a place of exceptional cultural and intellectual activity. Its reputation attracted many of the most exciting talents of the day, innovators in literature, art, science and philosophy whose impact on Euripides has often been noted.[1] The effect of this intellectually stimulating atmosphere on Euripides' style and themes has given his work a particular appeal to modern audiences and the *Bacchae* has been especially popular in the last 30 years or so. It is easy to see why. In modern popular culture, Dionysus has an immediate

appeal as the god of wild behaviour, of unrestrained drinking
and orgies, even though such 'divine decadence' is but one part
of the complex nature of the god of the *Bacchae*,[2] while thematically, in the gripping conflict between the charismatic and
unsettling god and his young opponent, the *Bacchae* effectively
combines the traditional motif of divine wrath at human disrespect with remarkably contemporary themes of masculinity and
femininity, the nature of religious belief, violence, and even
drugs and mental disturbance.

An ancient biographical tradition about Euripides exists,
but, like all such biography, it is untrustworthy because it relies
heavily on anecdotes and on the assumption that a poet's writ-
ings literally reflect his life.[3] It is, however, generally accepted
that in 408 he left Athens and, at the invitation of king
Archelaus, went to Macedon where he died in 406. Many critics
suspect that the descriptions of the natural world and even
elements of the cult of Dionysus in the *Bacchae* were influenced
by the surroundings of his last years. Later sources allege that
frustration at his fellow citizens' disdain for his plays impelled
him to seek voluntary exile so late in his life, but this is
doubtful. Great poets in the ancient world frequently received
invitations from kings who wanted to raise their court's
cultural prestige – Aeschylus had accepted a similar invitation
to Sicily some 50 years earlier – and Euripides' motivation for
departure need not have been pique at his reception by Athens.

Even so, it is true that, by strictly statistical criteria,
Euripides was less successful with audiences than were
Aeschylus and Sophocles, the other great tragedians of Athens.
Greek tragedies were performed at the Great Dionysia, an
annual competition among three playwrights chosen by the
state, who presented four plays at a time to the Athenian public.
From inscriptions listing the prize-winners, we learn that, in 31
competitions, Sophocles won first prize 18 times, and otherwise
always came second. By contrast, in 22 competitions, Euripides
won a mere five first prizes, one of which was awarded posthu-
mously in 405 or a little later for the set of plays that included
the *Bacchae* and *Iphigenia in Aulis*.[4] It would be wrong to
conclude from these bare statistics that the Athenians actively

disliked Euripides' plays. If they had, he would not have been able to present his plays at public expense year after year, while tradition has it that even Sophocles paid tribute to him in 406 when, at the announcement of the titles of plays accepted for performance at the Dionysia, the older playwright wore mourning dress to show sorrow for his rival's death.[5] But Euripides never seemed to win the unqualified admiration received by Sophocles, or by his predecessor Aeschylus, whose work acquired classic status right after his death. Why this was so, and why the *Bacchae* found a success relatively unusual for Euripides, is worth brief discussion.

Euripidean tragedy is traditional in its subject matter which, like that of his rivals, derives from a centuries-old body of mythology. That his work often explores transgression and violence, especially within families, is also unexceptionable for the genre of tragedy. The difficulties that ancient and modern critics have had with Euripides originate from certain tendencies in how he handles these transgressions. Tragic characters are commonly driven to act so as to transcend normal human moral principles, but even as they commit terrible crimes, they must generate emotions of recognition and sympathy among their audiences. Yet it was not enough merely to represent terrifying or lamentable acts for the audience's emotional stimulation. Greek tragedies are not merely the ancient equivalent of horror films or tearjerkers, because the conventions of the genre necessitated that they stimulate the audience intellectually as well as emotionally. Playwrights therefore had to create a context for the tragic action through which their audiences could reflect at some intellectual distance on the circumstances surrounding the violence they had witnessed.[6] As a way of enabling space for such reflection, tragedians before Euripides tended to create characters who, though credible and sympathetic for their audience, still remained a little remote. Aeschylus' predecessor Phrynichus provided a salutary warning to his fellow tragedians when he famously violated this balance between sympathy and distance in his historical tragedy on the sack of the Athenians' close ally Miletus: the audience was too close to the events and burst into tears en masse, eventually severely fining him for 'reminding them of their own troubles' (Herodotus 6.21). Tragedy walks a narrow tightrope between intense emotion and intellectual reflection and between making pathos real enough to engage the audience while reassuring them that it is ultimately someone else's pain, not theirs, a balancing act reflected in the disjunction between the dreadful events tragedy portrays and the formalised language which describes them.[7]

Euripides' handling both of intellectual and of emotional matters has often been criticised. Abundant references in his plays to contemporary philosophical speculation and a strong interest in experimental dramatic structures have brought him charges of irrelevance, disunity, and even plain incompetence, by ancient and modern critics alike, especially those of the nineteenth and earlier twentieth centuries. Emotionally, his tragic figures tend to be less remote (and potentially more disturbing) than those of Sophocles and Aeschylus because he portrays them with greater naturalism, psychologically and to some degree physically and linguistically.[8] As an additional cause for unease among audiences, his plays sometimes seem to endorse ways of thinking about the universe which make traditional belief in the gods problematic, while simultaneously he brings gods onto the stage who are portrayed in an unflattering (though, as Mary Lefkowitz has shown, not untraditional) manner, as resembling human beings in their worst characteristics. It is hardly surprising, then, that he was sometimes dubbed an atheist by his contemporaries and many modern critics have found themselves compelled to assume that Euripides was criticising traditional beliefs.[9]

The *Bacchae* undoubtedly bears many of these Euripidean intellectual and emotional hallmarks. Contemporary audiences are often struck by an apparent psychological realism in the portrayal of Pentheus, and elements of Cadmus' handling of Agave's madness at the end of the play have been compared with modern psychoanalytic practices.[10] Much of the dialogue between the actors is linguistically straightforward, while Tiresias' speech (266-327) draws on contemporary philosophical theories. Yet the *Bacchae* has never faced any of the complaints typically made by Euripides' critics. One reason for this must be its structural and linguistic clarity: Euripides traces multiple reversals of power between Pentheus and Dionysus throughout the play, from the early scenes in which Pentheus prevails to the god's final triumphant speech over Pentheus' torn body. The reversals are underlined by the repetition of certain words throughout the play.[11] Another reason may be the exceptional lyricism of the chorus, whose portrayal of ecstatic religion is astonishingly vivid. But above all, it is the complex and compelling figure of the god himself, who dominates this play more than any god in any other tragedy, which makes the *Bacchae* one of the most admired of all Greek tragedies, even though Euripides' attitude to him – respect for his power or condemnation of his malevolence? – has long been a central topic of critical discussion.

One of Euripides' favourite subjects was the relationship between women and men and the apparent tendency of women to damage men when given the opportunity. The theme is rooted in traditional tales. Menacing women are a staple of Greek myth, and as early as Homer the power of female sexuality to destroy male society was feared. The *Odyssey*'s faithful Penelope is a rare exception to the typical run of women who are represented by adulteresses like Helen and her murderous sister Clytemnestra. Since men need women to reproduce their line, they must accept them into their families, but their supposed destructive tendencies necessitate firm male control. A prime manifestation of this need for control is the expectation that women belong indoors, while men's realm is outside. Vase painting and tragic masks conventionally portray men with dark skins, denoting their lives in the open, while women are painted in white. Athenian texts frequently assume that a woman's place is in the home: ideally she should be 'least mentioned for praise or blame'.[12] Such seclusion was often more of an ideal than a reality since economic necessity would have driven poorer women out to work, and obviously men lived with their families inside the house,[13] but still societal expectations of women and men were given concrete expression by the division between men's and women's space. A female public presence was only acceptable in religious contexts:[14] evidence for women's attendance at tragic performances remains inconclusive, but even if, as I believe, they were present, it is inconceivable that they were more than a minority in the audience.[15]

Yet even though they stay at home, because they bleed and give birth,[16] women are closely connected with the irrational forces that lurk outside, beyond the civilised city of men and with the dangerous, unpredictable phenomena of the natural world that in Greek thought must be contained for fear of what they will do if left unchecked.[17] Through their physiological make-up, women's bodies offer a symbol of female vulnerability to penetration by physical desires and emotions (regarded by the Greeks as external influences)[18] that are equated with a more general absence of rationality which the Greeks ascribed to animals and nature. Moreover, women's physical weakness in relation to men can be characterised as moral weakness, and, when linked with women's 'penetrability', inadequate self-control. To lack self-control is to be enslaved to passions, and to be less than truly free: in a slave-owning society the distinction between slave and free is not merely a metaphor.[19] Further, the inferiority of women's social position will be intensified in any society like Athens in which the political privileges of citizenship depend on military service. In sum, perceptions of women's physical and mental limitations 'naturally' create limitations on their activities, which then help to 'prove' female inferiority and the necessity of male control.

The Athenian opposition between men and women was part of a more comprehensive Greek system of polarities: men versus women; reason versus emotion; Greek versus non-Greek; free versus slave; human versus animal; and civilisation versus nature.[20] For a free Greek male, in the dominant position in society, the status of free Greek male is the desired norm: all others are inferior. Women are inferior to men and non-Greeks are inferior to Greeks, and since each status can easily be assimilated to others on its pole, non-Greeks can be stereotyped as womanish and slavish because they are conceived as opposites to the ideal of the (rational, intelligent, strong and self-controlled) Greek free male. This tendency might somewhat antedate the wars with Persia (490-478 BCE), but the comprehensive rout of the Persians is used by the Greeks, and especially the Athenians, as a concrete proof of an all-round superiority.[21] Since Easterners are the quintessential non-Greeks and the *Bacchae* follows the general tendency in Greek myth to imagine Dionysus as a god who comes from the East, Euripides' Pentheus, a Greek male himself, sees him with typically Greek prejudice as an effeminate purveyor of a dangerous religion which must be suppressed before it destabilises his city's society.

It is not possible to claim that Euripides either supports or condemns these typical conceptions of women and non-Greeks in the *Bacchae* because of the nature of Athenian tragedy. Since tragedy offers a voice to those marginalised by the dominant culture – women, foreigners, slaves – the genre automatically seems to question the values of that dominant culture while ultimately tending to endorse the Athenian 'system'.[22] The women of the *Bacchae* are at first portrayed in scenes of peaceful beauty as they worship on Mount Cithaeron and belie Pentheus' suspicions that they are involved in illicit sexual activity, yet they cannot be seen as innocent victims because they also become killers. Are they killers because an essentially harmless activity was impiously interrupted by an intruder? Or are women by their nature simply too volatile to handle freedom 'away from the loom' (1236)? Dionysus is obviously not the effeminate foreigner of Pentheus' imaginings, his cult is not trivial, nor is Pentheus right to accuse him of promoting sexual immorality. The god is undoubtedly vindicated as Zeus' son and the object of a very important cult. But the outcome of the play, in which the Theban royal house is destroyed and Agave explicitly renounces all things Bacchic, makes an unqualified endorsement of the cult impossible. Thus in his portrayal both of women and of a cult that has a particular appeal to them, Euripides challenges the status quo but ultimately seems to affirm the dangers of dismantling it.[23]

Euripides at the Great Dionysia[24]

By the time Euripides wrote the *Bacchae*, the genre of tragedy had been established in Athenian cultural life for over a century. The play was presented at Dionysus' own dramatic festival, the Great Dionysia, a literary, artistic, religious, political and educational experience. It took place in mid- to late March and included worship of Dionysus, processions and sacrifices as well as artistic performance. In its heyday, the artistic part of the festival lasted five days: three were devoted to tragedy, and, on each, one dramatist would present three tragedies and one satyr play.[25] The festival also included contests between choruses who sang dithyrambs, a form of choral lyric poetry whose traditional theme was Dionysus: according to Aristotle, tragedy itself originated from the dithyramb (*Poetics* 1449a10).

The Dionysia blurred the divisions between private and public and professional and amateur. It was truly a festival of the whole Athenian people. The actors were professionals, but the choruses were ordinary male citizens. While the chief magistrate of Athens was responsible for its organisation, financing was divided between the state and individuals. From the mid-fifth century on, the state paid the actors and provided an honorarium for the poets, while wealthy individuals (*chorêgoi*)[26] financed the training of choruses, an act of generosity which would win them credit among the Athenian people. A board of ten judges – one from each Athenian tribe – awarded prizes to the productions.

Tragic drama is intimately connected with Athenian public life. Before the performances began, the ten generals of Athens poured libations to 'democracy, peace and good fortune', while youths who had been brought up at the state's expense because their fathers had died fighting for Athens marched in glory to their seats. Lists of honours conferred on the city's benefactors were also read aloud. In the fifth century, the tribute collected from imperial Athens' subjects was even paraded before the audience.[27] Such preliminaries are likely to have stimulated civic pride among the Athenians in the audience, and, though the private emotional and aesthetic dimensions of tragedy must not be overlooked, the highly political activities surrounding the performance may also have created expectations among the audience that public and political issues might be a part of what they were about to see. When Pentheus believes that Thebes is in danger, he attempts to save his city from threat by an outsider: any citizen would be expected to do likewise and his subsequent spectacular destruction is therefore natural material for discussion by all those in the audience who were engaged in civic life. Since Athens was a direct democracy, in which any male citizen could vote directly on his city's policies, the potential link between the theatre and politics in the broadest sense of the term is much stronger than it is in modern Western society.[28]

Tragedy also has a religious dimension. The plays were performed in honour of Dionysus whose priest had a prime seat in the front row. Yet what he would sometimes see was far from what a modern audience might consider an act of worship. The Dionysus who appears in Aristophanes' *Frogs*, though likeable, is cowardly and opportunistic;[29] in Euripides' *Bacchae*, he is a seductive killer. Particularly striking to those familiar with the assumptions about divinity which underpin Christianity is the apparent contradiction between the lying, cruel, ungrateful gods of myth and tragedy and the gods who were worshipped by thousands throughout Greece and, to judge from other literary genres,[30] were expected to protect their worshippers in return for their devotion. This contradiction has occasioned considerable debate in recent scholarship. Jon Mikalson argues that the gods of tragedy were not considered identical with those who were objects of worship in Greek cult but rather were one-dimensional literary constructs associated with a mythical society of long ago. Christiane Sourvinou-Inwood has strongly disputed Mikalson's claims and argues that the apparent contradiction between the gods of tragedy and of cult is an illusion caused by viewing Greek religion through a liberal Western perspective: since Greek religion has no devil, the gods must therefore be responsible for all parts of life, including its darker side, and it is this side of them that is represented by tragedy which, as she proposes, explores the uncertainty and unknowability of human life rather than criticising or condemning the gods. In tragedy, the gods are not cruel at random, but punish in accord with accepted principles of crime and punishment and, moreover, the fact that so many tragedies conclude with the establishment of a cult indicates that the gods of tragedy cannot easily be divorced from those of everyday cult.[31] That said, it is striking that writers such as Xenophanes, Plato and Euripides himself all show a degree of alarm about the portrayal of the gods in tragedy and myth which makes it difficult to accept that there is no disjunction between the gods of tragedy and those of real cult.[32] One reason for this continued contradiction is that in Greek religion – even, to some degree, in its non-literary incarnation – worship is less dependent either on divine morality or on sacred texts than is typical in Christianity.[33] Whereas the Christian conception of God is of one all-powerful, all-good being who must therefore be loved and worshipped by his people, the fact of the gods' power is central to Greek religion. To portray Dionysus' revenge is to acknowledge his power, whether or not it accords with human morality, while even the comic portrayal of Dionysus in the *Frogs* honours the god of comedy by making him a supreme object of laughter.[34]

The first recorded tragedy dates from 501 BCE, but the genre had presumably been evolving for some time previously. Aristotle states that tragedy originated when the leaders of the dithyramb became soloists engaging in dialogue with the chorus (*Poetics*, 1449a10). The claim that choral poetry lies behind tragedy is consistent with the fact that a second actor was not introduced until Aeschylus, while the chorus is usually on stage throughout nearly the entire drama, far longer than any one actor. Even in Euripides' day, only three speaking actors ever performed on stage at any one time. Since the number of individual characters in tragedies always exceeds three, the actors must take several parts each, an arrangement which seems to exclude the possibility of method acting or especially close identification between actor and character played. Vase paintings show that the (male) actors wore masks, long embroidered robes with sleeves and high boots.

The constant stage presence of the chorus – 15 members by Euripides' day – shows that they are an essential element of tragedy. By the later fifth century, dramatic interest had shifted to the individual actors through whose choices the plot of the play unfolded: the chorus had become more reactive than active, their role largely confined to songs offering their own perspective on events, or at most responding to the individuals whose actions are of central importance. The *Bacchae*, however, seems to revert to older tragic practice by giving prominence to the chorus whose collective presence both provides a picturesque representation of the Eastern worshippers of the god and reminds the audience of the god's other worshippers on Mount Cithaeron outside Thebes, whose terrible deeds are recounted by the two messenger-speeches. The apparent contrast between the visible 'good' Bacchantes and the invisible 'bad' ones is intriguing and replicates an ambiguity central to the religion portrayed by Euripides.

The Theatre of Dionysus where the play was probably first performed was located just above his temple on the hillside south-east of the Acropolis. Substantial remains of a theatre are visible today, but these are of a later date. The ancient theatre consisted of an area called the *orchêstra* ('dancing-place') which is associated with choral song and dance. Later theatres had a separate raised stage for the actors, but this may be a post-Euripidean development. Behind the orchestra was a wooden building called the *skênê*, 12 metres long and 4 high, which had a flat roof (*theologeion*) on which divine appearances on high could be made, a door in the middle and, at least for later plays, a backdrop extending from it on either side. This façade was both a piece of scenery which could be painted to denote a particular setting, and a sounding board to help the acoustics in the theatre. The building itself was a changing room for the actors and also represented any structure which the characters of the drama entered: in the *Bacchae*, the building represents Pentheus' palace. Two paths (*parodoi* or *eisodoi*) on either side led off the stage and served as roads to and from the city in which the drama was set.

The theatre held an audience of maybe 12,000-14,000 people seated around three-quarters of the orchestra. The view at the back of the theatre, some 60 metres above the orchestra, was restricted, and it is generally thought that the acoustics were reasonably good, though not as good as those, for example, in the later theatre at Epidaurus where dramatic performances are held to this day. Sight and sound were aided by the masks worn by the actors, which emphasised their faces – subtlety of expression is pointless in a huge arena – and may also have augmented their natural voices. The use of masks also helps to broaden the reference of the action, to suggest that what is happening is not only a particular occurrence but an exemplification of a particular tendency in human existence.[35] Violent action is never directly portrayed on stage, but instead a messenger reports what has happened. As in radio drama, imagination can be more effective than literal representation and given the limited facilities for special effects on the Greek stage, it is likely that even when earthquakes are portrayed on stage, as in the *Bacchae*, little or nothing literally happens to the set, but the audience must be directed by the words and possibly movements of the chorus and actors to imagine what is happening.[36] The performers must act with large gestures in order to be visible: similarly, tragedy handles the large themes of human existence such as family tensions, the role of women, or the relationship of men to gods, all of which feature in the *Bacchae*. There is little place for the smaller-scale themes of many modern plays or films and although Euripidean tragedy offers more realistic characterisation than some earlier tragedies, Greek tragedy is neither as realistic nor as intimate as our modern theatre often is.

Unlike that of many of his plays, the dramatic structure of Euripides' *Bacchae* is very conventional, and this has been taken as one of several indications that Euripides was influenced by earlier tragedy when he wrote the play.[37] Dionysus introduces himself to the audience in a prologue which is then followed by a song (*parodos*) by the chorus as they enter the stage. Then the plot gradually unfolds in five acts or 'episodes' in which the actors interact with one another in longer speeches and dialogue. Songs (*stasima*) sung and danced by the chorus to an accompaniment of wind instruments and perhaps drums separate the episodes from one another. The last stasimon is followed by the *exodos* in which the action of the play is concluded and the chorus leave the stage.

1. Euripides and the Greek Theatre

Though it is often obscured in modern translation and performance, tragedy is poetry, and there is a strong correlation between the type of poetry used and the type of tragic discourse presented. Iambic trimeter, the metre closest to normal speech rhythms, was the standard metre for actors' speech.[38] Various kinds of communication between actors in this metre were possible: monologues; extended dialogue including *stichomythia* ('speaking in lines') in which actors speak alternating lines in a somewhat stylised conversation; and *antilabe* in which more than one speaker shares an iambic line at moments of extreme excitement.

The chorus can converse with the actors in iambic trimeter, but their discourse commonly takes place in various sung lyric metres: particular metres are associated with different levels of emotional intensity. Actors can also communicate with the chorus in lyric metres. Notable in the *Bacchae* is the use of the Ionic rhythm, which, for an audience attuned to the subtleties of Greek poetic rhythms, would evoke the stereotypical East of luxury and decadence. The use of the trochaic tetrameter catalectic, a metre whose use in tragic dialogue antedates that of iambic trimeter, is another archaic feature.[39] The actors' language advances the action of the play: it is linear, logical and often influenced by rhetorical and other contemporary intellectual developments. By contrast, the language of the choral odes is generalised, lyrical and often obscure, full of poetic imagery and leaps in time and place. The chorus are not bound by time, so can open the play up beyond linear narrative, moving from present to past to future, in order to link the play with wider themes in myth or human experience: the 'timelessness' of choral lyric is particularly effective in the *Bacchae* when the chorus simultaneously prophesy and evoke Pentheus' death (977-1023). They can often represent the voice of the community and Greek ethical norms but can also be used by tragedians to highlight whatever aspects of the action they want at a particular moment, so that choral identity, unlike that of the actors, is often somewhat fluid. The chorus of the *Bacchae* is therefore a little unusual in having such a strong collective identity and relatively consistent characterisation as Eastern female followers of Dionysus. Given how frequently tragedians use their chorus to represent a Greek citizen body, this alien presence on stage may be deliberately unsettling, especially since they combine wild barbarian utterances with highly conventional maxims from familiar Greek wisdom on moderation and the importance of leading a life appropriate to mortals.[40] This mingling of Eastern and Western is emblematic of Euripides' portrayal of the god whom they follow, as we will see in Chapter 2.

2

Dionysus and Athens

Euripides' *Bacchae* portrays a foreign god who presides over wild rituals which culminate in the violent ripping apart of an animal (*sparagmos*) and its eating raw (*ômophagia*). It was once believed that all myth directly reflected, or at least could be traced back to, actual ritual, and the glamorous violence of Bacchic religion led some leading scholars of the play – among them, E.R. Dodds, whose commentary on the play is still fundamental reading – to believe that Euripides' portrayal of Dionysiac ritual reflected actual cult practice, even after the general theory that myth is an outgrowth of cult had been abandoned.[1] More recent study views Euripides' portrayal of the cult less literally and with an understanding that myth has a complex and not necessarily direct relationship to cult realities. The details of a mythical story need not be literally true or even derived from historical truth, but the story will have a symbolic truth for the societies in which it is told and may even generate its own ritual.

Reviewing the evidence for the historical cult of Dionysus is a problematic exercise. Much of the evidence for cult practice comes from sources outside Attica and later than Euripides: since Greek religion is highly regionalised and every city has its own forms of divine worship, one city's practice will not necessarily replicate that of Athens. The *Bacchae* itself is even a problem for a discussion of the realities of Dionysus-cult in Greece: due to its remarkable popularity, details of the cult portrayed by Euripides may themselves have influenced later cult practice.[2] Even with these caveats, however, the historical and archaeological records suggest on the one hand that the cult of Dionysus at Athens was significantly less sensational than its depiction by Euripides,[3] yet also that certain details from these and from earlier mythical representations of Dionysus imply that he was not creating a completely fictional account of Dionysus-worship in Greece but simply exaggerating certain inherent elements of the cult for dramatic purposes. There is a truth in Euripides' portrayal, but it is not a simple historical truth. Certain aspects of Dionysus are so constant in so many myths that they may surely be considered fundamental to the nature of the god in Greek religion, and this chapter will first consider Dionysus in a broader Greek context before discussing his role in Athenian religion and society. The last section of the chapter will discuss Dionysus in tragedies antedating the *Bacchae*.

Dionysus in Greek myth and religion

In myth, Dionysus always arrives from elsewhere: he is never imagined as having been in the city from the beginning. Earlier scholars assumed that myth reflected history and that he must be a foreign god from Thrace or Phrygia who was gradually incorporated (and tamed) by Greece, but when the Linear B tablets, dating from *c.* 1250 BCE, were deciphered some 50 years ago and found to be written in Greek, scholars were surprised to see the name of Dionysus on them.[4] Although his cult shows non-Greek influences, he was evidently a member of the earliest Greek pantheon. The sanctuary of Dionysus at Aya Irini on the island of Ceos is known for the continuity of its cult from the fifteenth century BCE down to Classical times, although details of the cult are obscure, and, for what it is worth, themes of Cretan art include elements such as wine and ivy, dancing women and snake handling, all of which are attested in later Dionysiac worship. The Dionysiac festival of the Anthesteria is celebrated in Ionia as well as Attica, and must have been established before the migrations from Attica to Ionia of *c.*1000 BCE.[5]

The idea that Dionysus comes from elsewhere is symbolically, rather than historically, true. He is the god of epiphany who appears and disappears, a trait seen as early as the Homeric

Hymn to Dionysus which begins with an 'appearance' of the god on the shore (*Hom. Hym.* 7.2). The *Bacchae* itself is full of Dionysiac epiphany, from his first appearance in Thebes through his disappearance at the earthquake scene and reappearance to the Chorus and Pentheus (604, cf. 645), his vanishing from Cithaeron (1057) and final reappearance in triumph (1330). As a god of epiphany, he is exciting and disruptive: he has a home in his city but he will always have a dimension beyond it as the god who is not fully contained or satisfied with one domain, the god who is always 'Other'.[6] This aspect of Dionysus is connected with another dominant motif of his myth: resistance. Bringing him into the city is typically not a simple matter of acceptance and appreciation: it is contested and always brings violence and suffering upon those who resist.

This aspect of Dionysus is central to the action of the *Bacchae*, which contains many motifs common to ancient myths of Dionysus' first visits to towns, and especially their ruling families: these include the god's revelation of his powers through miracles which are ignored by non-believers, violence against the god, his revenge, often through the infliction of madness, and repentance which comes too late. Homer (*Il.* 6.130ff.) recounts the story of Lycurgus of Thrace who attacked Dionysus and drove his nurses over Mount Nysa.[7] Dionysus escaped but Lycurgus was punished with blindness and death. A little later, Hesiod (cited by Apollodorus 2.2.2) tells the story of the three daughters[8] of king Proetus of Argos who were sent mad for refusing to honour Dionysus. Proetus called on the prophet Melampus to heal them, but Melampus demanded a third of the kingdom. When Proetus refused, his daughters grew even more agitated and the madness spread to the entire female population, who, like the Theban women in Euripides, went mad, left their homes for the wilds and killed their children. In Orchomenus, near Thebes, the three daughters of king Minyas preferred to stay at home with their weaving, rather than joining the other women of the city in Bacchic worship, and refused to recognise the god himself when he appeared before them. Only when Dionysus resorted to some alarming miracles, becoming a bull, lion or leopard and making their looms exude milk and nectar, did they join the cult, but it was too late: again, a mother tore her son to pieces, aided by her sisters.[9]

The Homeric Hymn to Dionysus focusses more on Dionysus' playfulness than on his violence but contains the same elements of failed resistance and Dionysiac miracles: pirates attempt to capture a stranger, who is the god, but cannot bind him and he sits smiling at his captors (cf. *Bacchae* 439, 648-9). The helmsman understands that he is a god and urges his release (17-24, cf. *Bacchae* 441-50), but he is ignored by the captain. But then a miracle happens: heavenly-smelling wine flows along the decks, and the mast burgeons with unstoppable vines and ivy and flowers and berries. Now the sailors believe, but, again, it is too late. Dionysus in the form of a lion springs upon the captain, and the sailors who leap into the sea turn into dolphins: only the helmsman is saved.[10] All of these myths tend towards the same conclusion. The god and his gifts are always accepted but only after a violent struggle.

It is not difficult to imagine how such myths might grow up around a god of wine.[11] Unlike Demeter's gift of wheat, wine is not an unmixed blessing for humanity. The plant from which wine is made demands human cultivation to tame it and will revert to the wild without continuous cultivation.[12] The product of the vines, if it is to benefit humanity, must then be tamed again in the time-consuming work of wine production. Even then, the process is not complete: pure wine is considered dangerously strong in Greek thought and must be tamed yet again by the admixture of water. Like its god, wine is both emblematic of civilised society and its potential destroyer. Wine brings many blessings and can liberate people from their care-worn lives by offering them a more exalted reality for a few hours[13] but it is easy to misuse it and precipitate disaster. Wine shares the colour of blood and thus can represent both human life and also death through violence: in fact, drunken transgression is a common motif in myth (e.g. Homer *Odyssey* 21.295-8). Ecstasy is not synonymous with drunkenness – part of Pentheus' mistake is that he equates the two – but it is an analogous state, so that it is natural that Dionysus also presides over ecstatic states. The theatre also brings respite from the problems of real life for a little: Dionysus is thus an appropriate patron for this too, especially since so much tragedy concerns change and reversal.[14] In short, Dionysus negates the normal, the everyday:[15] he can make everyday life more bearable with his blessings or he can use his powers on the sceptical or the hostile to make their lives far worse than normal.

Scholars often characterise Dionysus as a popular, rather than an aristocratic god: in myth, those in power resist the changes he brings because they have most to gain from the maintenance of the normality that he subverts. For those outside the 'establishment', such as non-aristocrats and women, he is an inspiring figure and it is sometimes suggested that the political changes of the seventh and sixth centuries stimulated the popularity of his cult. Homer makes little mention of Dionysus, but his presence is increasingly common in art, literature and cult of the seventh and sixth centuries, a period when the aristocratic families who had ruled Greece for centuries faced challenges to their authority from the 'tyrants', individuals who overturned their power with help from the people and ruled as kings in their place. The Homeric Hymn to Dionysus was composed in the seventh or sixth century BCE, while around 650 the poet Archilochus explicitly connects Dionysus, wine and poetic inspiration for the dithyramb.[16] Dionysiac revelry is frequently portrayed in Corinthian art at this time, while near Corinth, at Sicyon, king Cleisthenes offered particular honours to Dionysus in the 560s.[17] Sometime in the second half of the sixth century, tragedy takes its place beside the dithyramb in Dionysus' own dramatic festival. By 530/20, the portrayal of Dionysus with his bands of satyrs and maenads is fully developed in Athenian art, and the beginning of interest in Dionysiac mystery cults (see below) is often dated to the late sixth century. Since Dionysus in myth tends to challenge ruling families and help the less powerful, it is at least an interesting coincidence that his popularity grows at a time when the power of the traditional aristocratic families of Greece was decreasing.[18]

And yet, Dionysus cannot be categorised too easily. Though

he is the god of wine and festival, he remains detached from the festivities. The satyrs who surround him enjoy drunken sexual behaviour, but Dionysus is never drunk or portrayed in compromising positions. Festivals of Dionysus often included a parade of phalluses through the streets – even Athens' colonies were required to bring phalluses to the Dionysia every year – but even in the midst of this phallic celebration, the god himself is never portrayed with an erection.[19] The word ecstasy derives from the Greek *ekstasis*, literally a 'standing out or apart' and the god of ecstasy is the one who stands a little apart from the world around him. Dionysus is both thoroughly at home in the city, yet also the god of the wild, to whom the women make their mountain pilgrimage. As the god who comes and goes, who is present and absent, who is violent and soft and a mediating figure between male and female, who moves between the city and the countryside,[20] who offers a gift both beneficial and harmful, which he exemplifies and yet from which he remains detached, Dionysus exemplifies ambiguity. Like his gift of wine, Dionysus spans opposites.

While such characteristics are much more obvious in the Dionysus of myth, and especially tragedy, they occur in a milder form in the Dionysus of non-tragic literature and cult.[21] Some of his cult titles denote a god who is both dangerous and gentle to humans. In Sicyon, he is represented by two statues, one called Baccheios (the god of frenzy) and one called Lysios (the god of release). On Lesbos, he is 'eater of raw flesh' but 'mild' on Naxos.[22] Two fifth-century bone tablets read 'life/death/life, peace/war and truth/falsehood' along with an abbreviation of Dionysus' name.[23] Even the story of Dionysus' birth (already known to Herodotus) is marked by ambiguity. His father is Zeus, the king of the gods, his mother the mortal Semele, who was persuaded by Zeus' jealous wife Hera to ask her lover to appear in his true form to her. When Zeus appeared to her as lethal lightning, he rescued the embryo and implanted it in his thigh until the baby was born. Thus, uniquely, Dionysus has a male and a female mother.[24]

Most male gods tend to impregnate women and then abandon them. By contrast, Dionysus' relationship with women involves a more cooperative role as imagined leader of the rites performed by Maenads. Many forms of Dionysiac worship were open to both sexes, but it seems that the Maenads, whose name shares a root with the Greek word for madness (*mania*), were exclusively women.[25] Crazed violence, culminating in *sparagmos* of a wild animal and *ômophagia*, is integral to the mythical representation of Maenads and already Homer associates Dionysus with bands of maddened women (*Il.* 6.130ff.).[26] But the myth again only seems to represent a symbolic truth. While the myth imagines spontaneous outbursts of intense ecstasy, reality seems more prosaic: the archaeological record shows that, at least in historical times, the festival took place at a fixed time in the calendar, and while a few individuals may have experienced true ecstatic possession, the reality was probably less intense, as exemplified in the saying, 'Many are the narthex bearers but few are the Bacchae.' While visits to mountains are attested for Bacchic worshippers, there is no evidence that the more sensational parts of the myth reflect standard cult practice. Myth gives license to *imagine* what is *not* literally done, and the act of murder can clearly symbolise the disorder and danger which seem inextricably attached to the god's persona. Whether or not murder had ever been a literal part of the ritual is unanswerable, but, even if one could prove that the murders, especially of children, which occur so often in the myths of Dionysus reflected ancient practice, it would say nothing about the cult in Euripides' time.

Moreover, *sparagmos* was never the standard means of sacrifice to Dionysus, and only once in the entire inscriptional record of Dionysus' cult is there a reference to *ômophagion*, on an inscription from Miletus dated nearly 200 years after the *Bacchae* itself.[27] It mentions a procession to the mountain and states that no one is allowed to 'throw in the *ômophagion*' before the priestess has done so on behalf of the city. This would indicate that, at least in Miletus, cult activity was more regulated than that described by Euripides and was controlled by the city, rather than being a spontaneous expression of rebellion against it. Thus current scholarly opinion interprets the *sparagmos* less as a literal practice than as an imaginary act with several potential connections with the social conditions under which the female worshippers of Dionysus lived. It has been variously suggested that the *sparagmos* is an expression of female power, briefly but intensely experienced, or conversely that in its strangeness it represents the marginal position of women in their society.[28] What does seem clear is that it belongs to the large category of rituals in Greece which affirm the normal social order by a brief period of abnormality.[29] In normal sacrifice, a domesticated animal is ritually selected, cut up and cooked and eaten, whereas the *sparagmos* involves a supposedly spontaneous attack on a wild animal, which is torn apart and eaten raw by women away from their normal dwelling place within their homes in the city.[30] Raw meat itself is sometimes offered to Dionysus, although not through *sparagmos*, and such an offering has been similarly interpreted as a brief violation of the normal social order.[31] Since the Dionysus of myth and tragedy is so strongly associated with violations of social norms, such offerings provide one common link between the god of tragedy and the god of cult.

So while Euripides' version of Dionysiac ritual is a sensationalised portrayal, there is undoubtedly common ground between his conception of the cult and actual practice. If women's ordinary lives were somewhat restricted and isolated, then the brief period as Maenads, supposedly led by Dionysus himself, in which they were allowed to break out of normality away from the constraints of the home and the city – though only in terms strictly defined by that city – and to live in a purely female society would clearly be valuable to them.[32] The *sparagmos* during that time would be an important symbol of the quality of their time away from the ordinary, whether it was purely imaginary, whether it was symbolised by the handling of raw meat, or whether it was ever at all close to Euripides' dramatised vision of the ritual. Certainly the *Bacchae* seems to incorporate a number of less sensational, but genuine elements of the Dionysiac experience, such as torchlight, loud music, dancing and head-tossing.[33] A sleepless and exhausting night dancing in the imagined presence of the god could obviously bring its participants into a sense of relaxation and well-being.[34]

2. Dionysus and Athens

Whether this experience was, as popularly believed, fuelled by wine and sex, whether it was a sedate day out, or whether it was somewhere in between and varied dramatically from group to group,[35] it is by definition temporary, and, just as their divine leader comes and goes, so the women leave the city and become Other, but will return again to normality.

The cult of Dionysus at Athens

The Athenian Dionysus is a god of wine and vine miracles, wild nature, ecstatic possession, dance, masking and disguise, and mystic initiation.[36] There is no clear evidence for Maenadic ritual within the borders of Attica, although later sources mention a joint celebration on the slopes of Parnassus between the Thyiads of Delphi and Athenian women (Plutarch *Moralia* 249e-f, Pausanias 10.4.3). Dionysus was, however, central to a number of festivals in Athens which are worth brief discussion because there is some unanimity in their portrayal of the god and because there are clear thematic connections between them and the Maenadic rites represented by Euripides.

The Lenaea took place in Athens in January. Its precise structure remains uncertain, probably because it was eclipsed in Classical times by the Great Dionysia which took place two months later,[37] but its origins were certainly ancient. It comprised procession, sacrifice and dramatic performance in honour of Dionysus. Since its name seems to be derived from the Greek word *lênai*, meaning 'madwomen', it may once have contained a Maenadic element. The festival is sometimes thought to be portrayed on a group of vases which show women worshipping a primitive statue of Dionysus made from a mask and a pillar along with occasional scenes of *sparagmos* (ARV[2] 583, 34), but without more evidence the significance of these pictures must remain uncertain.[38]

More is known of the Anthesteria which celebrated the new vintage and the arrival of Dionysus in February.[39] The first of its three days, *Pithoigia*, or 'Opening of the Wine Jars', was filled with preparation. In the evening, jars full of the new wine were taken to the sanctuary of Dionysus in the Marshes and the day culminated with a tasting. The second day (*Choes*, 'Jugs') was full of drinking contests for everyone, including slaves and children, and parties, but they were not joyous. The drinking was not the communal festivity of the symposium but silent, and each person sat at his own separate table. Contrary to normal custom, hosts of parties provided no wine but only garlands and dessert, and guests had to bring their own wine. It was also a day when spirits were thought to wander around and myths were told of the darker side of Dionysus.

The Athenians explained the paradoxically sombre festivities through the myth of Orestes who came to Athens when still polluted with matricide: as a stranger, he had to be entertained, yet as a murderer he had to be shunned. The ambiguity which has been considered fundamental to Dionysus' mythical persona is striking here. At sunset on *Choes*, the drunk Athenians went to the sanctuary of Dionysus in the Marshes – only open on this day – where 14 *gerarai* (old women) performed secret rituals under the control of the wife of the *archôn basileus*, the Athenian magistrate in charge of the oldest religious cults at Athens. The evening probably ended with a marriage procession back to Athens so that the archon's wife could undergo a sacred marriage, supposedly to the god himself, in the Boukolion, a building in the centre of the city. The incorporation of Dionysus into the city each year is partly a supposed memorial of the god's first arrival in the city (as recalled by certain myths discussed below) and also a means by which the city can renew and unite itself in regular communal celebration. The last day of the Anthesteria is *Chytroi* ('Pots'), on which grains boiled with honey – supposedly the first food eaten after the primal flood – represent new courage and life, though death is not banished, as sacrifices to Hermes of the underworld are performed. Girls also participate in a swinging contest (*aiôra*), whose aetiology is the story of Erigone, daughter of king Icarius, who hanged herself in sorrow at her father Icarius' murder,[40] but even as the children swing, life prevails and spring is welcomed. The Dionysus of the Anthesteria presides over festivity but also irregularity, just as his wine is both beneficial and dangerous.

2. Dionysus and Athens

The theatrical Dionysus was given especial prominence in Athens in the Lenaea and above all in the Rural[41] and City (Great) Dionysia. This festival honoured Dionysus Eleuthereus, and its preliminaries were based around an ancient cult statue of Dionysus which the Athenians had supposedly carried off from the border town of Eleutherae.[42] This statue was taken out of Dionysus' temple on the southern slope of the Acropolis near the theatre and carried to the Academy, a grove outside the city on the way to Eleutherae, where hymns and sacrifices were performed before the god's triumphant return through the middle of the city by torchlight.[43] The main part of the festival was, of course, drama and Dionysus' two aspects of pleasurable festivity and darkness are exemplified in his two theatrical genres. Comedy offers exceptional licence for festivity and even obscenity and abuse of the powerful, while the darker genre of tragedy presents various transgressions of human norms to an audience.[44]

Many scholars contrast the relatively benign Athenian Dionysus with a violent Theban Dionysus[45] but certain myths surrounding his introduction to Attica show patterns of resistance to the god which closely resemble those found in Theban myth. King Icarius[46] received the gift of a vine from Dionysus, but when he invited his neighbours to taste the new drink, they became drunk and violent, and thought that he had poisoned them, so mutilated his body and flung it into a well. But, in an apparent sequel to the story, Pegasus of Eleutherae wished to bring Dionysus' statue to the Athenians, and the Delphic oracle reminded them that the wine god had previously been in Icarion. The Athenians were understandably hesitant about inviting him in, but when Dionysus used his powers for miraculous punishment, this time in causing unceasing erections in the male populace, they followed the oracle's advice to build phalluses and carry them in procession to honour the god. Moreover, the unmixed wine that had caused such trouble for Icarius was finally under control as the god taught king Amphiction to mix it with water.[47] This story explains the preliminaries to the Great Dionysia: bringing the god home to the heart of the city is an act of whole-hearted and unconditional welcome. Dionysus demands no less (cf. *Bacchae* 208-9). While these myths and others are only preserved by sources much later than Euripides, myths tend to be forgotten if they are no longer meaningful to their audience. That such stories are still found in late writers may be an indication of the continuity of what Dionysus represented to the Athenians.

So, in the mythological tradition, Athens, like other cities, had experienced difficulties with Dionysus. Yet there may indeed be some distinction between Athenian Dionysus and the Theban god. Dionysus has his own places in Athens and official times in the Athenian year when he presides over abnormality, whether in the joyous naughtiness of comedy or the serious transgressions of tragedy. To give Dionysus a delineated space and time to execute his powers enables Athens to incorporate without danger a god who is otherwise associated with a dangerous lack of control.[48] Moreover, Athenian versions of myth commonly contrast Athenian success with Theban disaster: so many tragedies focus on the murderous and incestuous house of Labdacus that Isocrates can claim Athenian superiority because, unlike Thebes, incest and murder have never been typical of the city. It is understandable that at a festival of their own well-managed Dionysus, the Athenians might be amenable to watching Theban destruction caused by handling Dionysus badly.[49]

Dionysus and the afterlife

From at least the sixth century, Dionysus is associated with the underworld, and since the association is so frequent around the ancient world, many scholars accept its presence at Athens as well, even though evidence for it there is less clear.[50] Heraclitus equates Dionysus with Hades and visits of Dionysus to the underworld are frequent in myth.[51] In many parts of the ancient world, tombs were decorated with Dionysiac figures and emblems, and some tombs have yielded a series of inscribed golden leaves, which seem to be intended as guides for the dead to negotiate their way through the underworld and find rebirth under Dionysus' aegis.[52] Thus Dionysus has another incarnation as the object of mystery cult. Mystery cults contrast with the normal public religion of Classical Greece by offering a personal relationship with the god and a blessed afterlife to anyone willing to undergo initiation.[53] Initiation rituals typically include extensive preparation, special clothing[54] and abstinence from food or sex. The ritual itself often contains some symbolic suffering or fearful experience which is joyously dispelled by a later part of the ritual: frequent are moves from darkness to light, as a symbolic enactment of the path from death to afterlife.[55] The gods of mystery cult always offer a close relationship with their worshippers, but Dionysus' relationship with his initiates is especially intense. First, in his rites, both god and worshipper become 'Bacchus', merging with one another in a manner unusual in Greek religion.[56] Second, and even more importantly, in the myths which reflect his persona as a god of mystery cult, he is a god who dies and even has a grave at Delphi (Plutarch *Moralia* 365a). Thus he is a god who undergoes a uniquely human experience and, through his own rebirth, is a role model for initiates seeking a happy afterlife. In this incarnation, like that as the god who soothes human cares with his gift of wine, this god is unusually close to human beings.

The Dionysus who dies is generally known as Dionysus Zagreus and myths associated with him have been connected with so-called 'Orphism'.[57] The term derives from the mythical singer Orpheus, famed for his failed attempt to rescue Eurydice from the underworld and eventual death, like Pentheus, at the hands of Maenads. Orphics typically detached themselves from mainstream society through extreme asceticism and by espousing cosmogonical and theological beliefs notably different from the standard versions found in Hesiod or Homer.[58] Although few extensive or early sources for the Orphic account of Dionysus exist, a number of passing references to the myth indicate that it may have had relatively early currency and was familiar in Athens: in this version, Zeus raped his mother Rhea-Demeter, from whom was born Persephone, whom Zeus raped in the form of a snake. From her was born Dionysus, whom Zeus made ruler of the world. But the jealous Hera sent the

Titans to distract the child with toys and while he was looking into a mirror, they dragged him from the throne, tore him up, and boiled, roasted and ate him. Zeus then killed the Titans with his thunderbolt but from the rising soot sprang men: hence humans are natural rebels against Zeus but blessed with a spark of divinity from Dionysus. Zeus then gathered Dionysus' remains and he was reborn.[59] Plato speaks of Dionysiac mysteries performed according to the books of Orpheus which bring liberation from an 'ancient guilt' and his words have been interpreted as a reference to the Titans' murder of Dionysus in which human beings are implicated through their origin.[60] Since this story makes reference to a number of initiatory practices, it has been thought to indicate a connection between the incarnation of Dionysus who dies and lives again and initiation into mystery cult which brings a happy afterlife through rebirth under the god's auspices.[61] The story may also offer a partial pattern for the Pentheus story, and for other Dionysiac stories of murder and *sparagmos*, and some scholars interpret Pentheus' fate in the play as a failed initiation (below, pp. 95, 100).

Dionysus in tragedy before the *Bacchae*

The Greek proverb 'Nothing to do with Dionysus' is often quoted to support the assertion that tragedy once focussed exclusively on the god (or at least that the Athenians believed that this was so). Whatever the truth of this may be,[62] a few titles of plays attributed to early tragedians do suggest Dionysiac content, although their actual remains are uninformative. Thespis, traditionally Athens' first tragedian, is said to have written a *Pentheus*, while plays called *Bacchae* are attributed to Sophocles and a number of less well-known tragedians, both before and after Euripides' *Bacchae*: the *Bacchae* of Xenocles took first prize in the contest of 415 BCE.[63] Aeschylus found particular inspiration in the myths of Dionysus, and ascribed to him are plays called *Bacchae*, *Pentheus*, and *Semele*, while, according to an ancient commentator, his *Xantriae* portrayed Pentheus' death on Cithaeron. Which, if any, of these plays formed a connected trilogy we do not know (the evidence is very fragmentary), but it is certain that he composed a tetralogy on King Lycurgus, Dionysus' persecutor in *Iliad* 6.130ff. Few fragments are extant and fewer are revealing, but even such scanty remains contain motifs which find close parallels in the *Bacchae*.[64] The *Edoni* included the capture and interrogation of Dionysus, who is mocked, perhaps by the king, for effeminacy (fr. 60-2; cf. *Bacchae* 453f.), and the imprisonment of Dionysus' followers by King Lycurgus and their subsequent miraculous release followed by damage to the king's palace (58; cf. *Bacchae* 443f., 576ff.). The chorus, however, was composed of Lycurgus' subjects (fr. 57), not Dionysus' worshippers, whose presence on stage must remain uncertain.

A fragment of the Roman poet Naevius' *Lycurgus* features a raid on farms like that of *Bacchae* 748 and the two may share a common source in Aeschylus. Aeschylus' plot may lie behind the story of Lycurgus reported by Apollodorus (3.5.1): in this, Dionysus' revenge on the king sends him mad so that he kills his son while thinking that he is striking at a vine. His crime makes the land all around sterile and an oracle orders the Edonians to take him to Mount Pangaeus in Thrace where he is torn apart by wild horses. Thematic parallels with the *Bacchae* are obvious.[65]

The ancient summary of the play preserved in the text of Euripides' *Bacchae* claims that its story followed that of Aeschylus' *Pentheus*, and Aeschylus' *Eumenides* 24-6 states that Dionysus 'led the Bacchantes in war, and contrived for Pentheus death like a hunted hare'. On vases, Pentheus is always portrayed in male dress and with weapons, contrary to the plot of the *Bacchae*, so it is possible that the unarmed journey to Cithaeron in female clothing was one of Euripides' innovations in the tale.[66] Iconographical evidence has also led most scholars to believe that Pentheus' murder by his mother was also Euripides' invention (although child murder recurs frequently in Dionysiac myth) since no vases name his mother as his murderer and in the earliest representation of his death, *c*. 520-10 BCE, his killer is a Maenad macabrely called Galene, or 'Calm'.[67] The essential action of the *Bacchae* would be largely complete without Cadmus and Tiresias, and thus many commentators surmise that they too are Euripides' own addition to the story of Pentheus and Dionysus. It is time now, however, to turn to what Euripides made of the literary and religious material he had inherited.

3

Analysis of the *Bacchae*

In a prologue speech typical of Euripidean drama (1-63), the god Dionysus explains the background to the events which are about to unfold. Of central importance is his identity as the son of Zeus, and the punishment he will inflict on all those in Thebes who doubt his divinity. He has disguised himself as a mortal priest of Dionysus so that he can mingle with them and encourage them to join his worship. He points out the memorial of his mother Semele who was blasted by Zeus' lightning: even now, the place smoulders with Zeus' fire. Cadmus, Semele's father, has designated the spot as a holy shrine and he commends his action (10).[1]

Thebes is the first Greek city which he has visited with his band of Eastern followers. Many Thebans already worship him, but his mother's sisters have denied his divinity and claim both that Semele invented the story of her pregnancy by Zeus to hide sexual impropriety with a mortal lover and that her death was Zeus' punishment for the lie. This is a sacrilegious slander against his parents and, in his anger, Dionysus has sent mad not only his aunts but the entire female population of Thebes so that they have left their homes for Mount Cithaeron. Dionysus is obdurate: the city has no choice but to accept his divinity (39).

Dionysus then explains the succession of power at Thebes: old Cadmus has given the kingdom to his grandson Pentheus, the son of Semele's sister Agave. Like his aunts, Pentheus denies his cousin's divinity and is implacably hostile to him. The god promises pitched battle between his followers and Pentheus if necessary (52; cf. p. 35 above) before commanding the Chorus to play their drums around Pentheus' house while he withdraws to Cithaeron.

The *parodos* of the Chorus of Lydian women follows (64-167).[2] They sing in honour of Dionysus in the metre and style of a traditional cult hymn in which they describe the practices and beliefs of his cult. They express total belief in their god, whose rituals in the mountains bring them holiness, peace and intense happiness (72ff.). As is traditional in the genre of the dithyramb, they tell the story of Dionysus' extraordinary birth; how Zeus rescued him from his lightning blast and sewed him into his thigh to save him from his hostile wife Hera (89ff.). In ecstatic, repetitive language they invite Thebes to wear ivy crowns and fawnskins in the new god's honour and to share in his rituals. Only a faint hint of something more sinister might emerge from the description of the thyrsus[3] as 'violent' and the worshippers as 'maddened' (115, 118-19) and even the fawnskins imply that the religion incorporates a degree of savagery.[4] Ecstatic drumming is also important in Dionysiac worship, and they describe the invention of the drum by the Corybantes.[5] They briefly mention the hunt and 'raw-flesh-eating delight' of the subsequent *sparagmos* (135f.) but lay more emphasis on a scene of miraculous worship during which the ground pours forth milk, wine and honey while the god cavorts among them (141ff.).

The first episode begins at 170. Tiresias, the aged blind prophet of Thebes, appears on stage and calls old Cadmus to join him. His costume marks him as a convert to Dionysus and the cult has so excited him that he is not even accompanied by his usual attendant to guide his steps. Cadmus too wears Bacchic costume but he is a novice and anxiously (and slightly comically) requests instruction; though he professes willingness to dance all night (187) he wonders if they could save some energy by taking a carriage to Cithaeron. But Tiresias assures him that Dionysus will give them strength and that a journey on foot shows greater respect for him. They are the only Theban males to participate in the ritual and believe that this shows their unique good sense (195-6). Tiresias, with Cadmus' assent, condemns those who rely excessively on intellect (*to sophon*)[6] when considering religion. Such an approach is dangerous to individual and communal well-being and it is better to accept religious matters without argument. The god must have honour from everyone (206f.).

Now appears a third figure, whose appearance is flustered (212f.). This is Pentheus, who is appalled at the mania running riot in his city. He immediately characterises the religion as a mere pretext for drinking and sexual misconduct among the women, and Dionysus as a 'new' and therefore false god (219ff.). He has tried to nip the cult in the bud by jailing some of the worshippers and threatens to hunt the rest down from the mountain. But there is now a new and worrying development: the arrival of an effeminate young Easterner who lures the young into immorality under the pretence of religion. He threatens to decapitate him if he persists in peddling the cult and pours scorn on the story of Dionysus' birth. At last he notices the dreadful wonder of Cadmus and Tiresias decked out as Bacchantes. His grandfather looks as though he has lost his wits and Pentheus instantly blames Tiresias, accusing him of having brought the god to Thebes for personal gain. He even warns him that it is only through respect for his age that he does not imprison him immediately (248ff.).

In an important speech (266-327), Tiresias attempts to change Pentheus' mind. First, Dionysus is one of the two essential elements of human life. The goddess Demeter is grain or the giver of grain – the distinction between the divinities and what they embody is blurred – and Dionysus is her counterpart as (the god of) wine. Unlike the Chorus, Tiresias does not believe that Dionysus was literally born from Zeus' thigh but explains the story through word-play. When Hera wanted to expel the infant from Olympus, Zeus protected him by fashioning a new baby from a piece (*meros*) of the sky and giving it as a hostage to Hera. Eventually people believed that he had been sewn into Zeus' thigh (*ho mêros*) when really he had been Hera's *homêros*, or hostage (286ff.).

Dionysus is not only a god as good as any other but maybe even greater because, along with his own abilities, he possesses others traditionally ascribed to other gods. Like Apollo, he can give the gift of prophecy and, like Ares, he can influence armies, sending fear through them so that they run from the battlefield

(298-305). Dionysus can subdue any human force: neither physical nor political power can conquer the god. What he cannot do,
however, is harm the women of Thebes morally, because an individual's reaction to Dionysus depends on what he brings to the
encounter in the first place. A truly moral (*sôphrôn*) woman
cannot be corrupted by his revels. As a final inducement (319f.),
Tiresias appeals to Pentheus' sense of fairness – he enjoys
receiving respect, and Dionysus is the same – and warns him
that denial of the god of madness is itself insanity.

Cadmus agrees with Tiresias in begging Pentheus to be
sensible and worship the god. Even if, he says, Dionysus does
turn out to be a fraud, Pentheus should worship him nonetheless because it is such a great coup to be said to have a god in
the family, especially since they have already been victims of
divine hostility, when Pentheus' cousin Actaeon was torn apart
by his own hunting dogs (330-42).[7] He stretches out his hand
to his grandson but Pentheus shakes it off as though the
Bacchic madness is contagious. Now even more convinced that
Tiresias is responsible for his troubles, he threatens to destroy
his oracular seat at Delphi (345f.) and orders his subjects to
hunt down the corrupting stranger. Tiresias sees that
Pentheus is hopelessly locked in his 'madness' (358-9) and
gives up. Instead, he invites Cadmus to accompany him in
praying that the god not bring them *penthos* (grief) as a
punishment for Pentheus' folly.

In the first stasimon (370-432), the Chorus reiterate in lyric
poetry the conflicts of the previous episode. For them, the god is
joyously benign and any opposing view is unholy arrogance.
They agree with Tiresias' distinction between mere intellect
and truer wisdom, as they riddlingly claim: '*to sophon ou
sophia*' or 'what [seems as though it] is wise is not truly wise'
(395). Their idea of wisdom is an unconditional submission to
Dionysus and a vision of human mortality which makes ambition foolish: life is short and there is no point in conceiving
grand plans (397f.). They express a desire to go revelling to
Cyprus and other places where Aphrodite is worshipped or to
the Muses in northern Greece (401ff.): through these divine
metonymies, they express the association of wine with love and

singing. Their Bacchus brings his gifts of wine and cult to rich and poor alike. A life with him pursuing humble goals is preferable to any grander plans (427f.).

In the second episode (434-518), Pentheus meets the stranger. He is described as 'prey' and a 'beast' (434, 438), hunted down by Pentheus' men. The attendant who brings him to his master is surprised that he neither resisted nor ceased to smile[8] and is embarrassed at having to treat him as a prisoner (437f.). Even more strangely, the women whom Pentheus had imprisoned have miraculously been released. The servant clearly suspects that the stranger is responsible, but does not go as far as Cadmus and Tiresias in urging Pentheus to change his mind.

At 451, Pentheus inspects the stranger of whom he has heard so much. He is fascinated with his long hair and pale skin and considers them symbolic of the sexual irregularity with which he tempts the Theban women (455f.). In a passage of *stichomythia*, Pentheus interrogates him about his purpose in coming to Greece. In spite of the growing evidence for Dionysus' divinity, Pentheus continues to deny that he is Zeus' son and yet he is curious about his rituals. Since it is a mystery cult, the stranger refuses to divulge any secrets and Pentheus, still self-possessed at this stage, takes this as an attempt to trick him into wanting to know more (470-5). In fact, the stranger scarcely needs to encourage Pentheus' interest, since his fascination with Dionysiac ritual and conviction that it is merely a cover for immorality or a religion for foolish barbarians is manifested in a barrage of questions.

Until 491, the two seem equally matched: they trade insults and each uses the other's words against him. Pentheus threatens him with punishment for his tricks (*sophismata*): the stranger promises Pentheus punishment for his ignorance. But at 492 the stranger begins to lead Pentheus into explicit impiety by asking him what he plans to do to him. It is important to remember that Pentheus believes that the stranger is simply a human being. To Pentheus' threats that he will cut off his hair, take his thyrsus and imprison him, the stranger responds (492-8) with a baffling mixture of warning (his hair is holy), passivity

("Take the thyrsus yourself"), and indifference ('The god will free me whenever I want'). Pentheus does not understand a deep menace in his responses: his hair is grown *for the god* and Dionysus is 'where he is' (502). His opponent is a god, but, far from recognising this, Pentheus ends the interview by commanding his men to seize him. His assertion of superior power (505) is illusion, and his ignorance is encapsulated in one of their last exchanges: to the stranger's accusation that he does not know who he is, Pentheus responds literally by stating his name and lineage. Still imagining that he is in charge, Pentheus orders the stranger to be imprisoned in the stables while he threatens the Bacchae with slavery (511f.)[9] but the stranger has the last word: 'You wrong us as you lead Dionysus into prison.' This is no figurative statement.

The second stasimon (519-75) is another hymn to Dionysus. The Thebans are reminded that it is their duty to accept this Theban god whose divine birth is contrasted with Pentheus' earth-born ancestry (537ff.).[10] To be earth-born in Greek thought is to resemble the earth-born Giants, the enemies of the Olympian gods who fought Zeus and were defeated: the comparison may hint at Pentheus' ultimate fate. Not knowing that their god is among them, the Chorus pray that he come from afar and punish his enemy (550ff.).

In the long third episode (576-861) Dionysus reveals real power. His divine voice is heard off stage, in a frantic dialogue with the Chorus, from whom we learn that an earthquake is destroying part of Pentheus' palace (587f.). Dionysus also reawakens the fire at Semele's tomb in a terrifying display at which his followers cower (597ff.). But, at 604, the stranger returns to the stage and speaks reassuringly to them, and they express joyous relief at their protector's escape. To them he is kind, but for Pentheus he has little sympathy as, with amused contempt (616f.), he describes his first clear victory over him. When the king tried to bind him, he eluded him easily, as he had promised (614, cf. 498), and sat quietly watching Pentheus' increasingly desperate efforts to tie up, not the stranger, but a bull, an incarnation of the god which will reappear later (618f., cf. 922). When Semele's tomb began to burn,

Pentheus became even more flustered, believing that his house was burning. The stranger claims uncertainty as to what happened next, but suspects that the god made a phantom of the stranger on which Pentheus vainly pounced until he was worn out (629ff.). And so the stranger slipped away and rejoined the Chorus.

Pentheus reappears at 643. The miracles have not changed his mind, nor is he mollified by the stranger's 'I told you so' of 649. He orders his men to bar the city and to the stranger's reply that gods are not deterred by bars, he merely blusters: the stranger is 'wise, wise, except where one should be wise' (*sophos*, 655). But now a messenger from Cithaeron appears. The marvels he has seen have affected him, but he is nervous to proceed because he has experienced Pentheus' rough tongue in the past (669f.). Pentheus assures him he will be safe, especially if his information enables even harsher charges to be laid against the leaders of the cult.

The messenger, a herdsman, was looking after his cows when he met the bands of women led by Pentheus' mother and aunts. Some were relaxing, others were performing rituals, but none was out of control or having drunken sexual encounters (677ff.). When they heard his cattle, the women leapt up, 'a wonder to see' for their order (693). Their unity with nature was remarkable: snakes licked their cheeks and they suckled the young of wild animals. Their thyrsi dripped with honey and brought forth wine and milk from the ground (694ff.). Such a sight, he says, would have converted even Pentheus. The herdsmen were impressed and unsettled by the wonders but eventually one plausible talker persuaded them to do Pentheus' bidding and hunt the women. They lay in ambush until the women began their worship: even the beasts and the whole of nature joined the revelry (726f.).

When the men leapt on the Bacchae, they repelled their attack and turned on their cattle. The mountain became a butcher's yard as young women ripped huge bulls apart with their bare hands (728ff.). Then they ran over the plains, destroying everything in their path and even snatched their children out of their own homes. In their exalted state they were invulnerable (748ff.): they balanced household utensils on their shoulders without dropping them and carried fire in their bare hands without getting burned. They were even impervious to the men's weapons, while doing damage to their attackers with their deadly thyrsi in a perverse rout of men by women, 'not without some god' (764) in the speaker's opinion. At last, they returned to the streams and washed themselves.

The messenger urges Pentheus to welcome Dionysus now that his power is so clear, but he is even more determined to rid Thebes of the Bacchic infection. He threatens to use his army, since Greek men simply cannot suffer such indignities from women (778ff.). Pentheus and the stranger briefly seem to reach stalemate as Pentheus threatens and the stranger condemns his threats as futile and dangerous (787-801.) At 802, the stranger seems to capitulate, by offering to deliver the women to him. Pentheus is suspicious and reiterates threats of military action, but the stranger calls him back with an irresistible offer (810): would he like to see what the women are doing on the mountain? As in the earthquake scene, the stranger seems to take pleasure in making Pentheus appear ridiculous. When Pentheus expresses enthusiasm for seeing the women *in flagrante*, the stranger feigns surprise that he would wish to see something disturbing and Pentheus must agree: of course, it would be terrible to see them drunk (811f.).

The stranger has his prey in hand and he drops his bombshell: to avoid the fate of the herdsman and his fellows, Pentheus must be camouflaged in women's clothing (821). Though he refuses at first, under the stranger's determined campaign of reassurance that he will not be ridiculed and warning that he can reach the women in no other way, his distaste for his new costume gradually diminishes. By 830, he is reconciled enough to seek instruction on what to wear and how to wear it. By 842, he has been convinced, or convinced himself, that any sartorial embarrassment is better than being bested by women. When Pentheus leaves the stage, the stranger prophesies his death, invoking Dionysus, who is 'not far away' to send him mad and prove the existence of Dionysus son of Zeus (849ff.).

The third stasimon (862-910) once more meditates on

3. Analysis of the Bacchae

Dionysiac religion. The Chorus prophesy certain punishment for mortals who transgress established divine law and again praise a peaceful and unambitious life (902-11). However, a more disturbing note is injected by the apparent statement that Dionysiac wisdom (*sophon*) enjoins revenge over enemies (877-81 = 897-901: cf. below, pp. 69-70).

The fourth episode (912-76) begins as the stranger calls Pentheus out of the house. In his new costume, he resembles one of his aunts: moreover, his mental state has changed along with his appearance as he sees double and sees the stranger as a bull. The stranger assures him that the god is 'with him' and that he sees as he should (917ff.). Like his grandfather earlier in the play, Pentheus is obsessed with Bacchic authenticity and the stranger acts as his lady's maid and instructor (925ff.). But even in this altered state, Pentheus is still essentially the same: he imagines lifting up Mount Cithaeron by himself, and looks forward to seeing the sexual antics of Dionysus' worshippers (945ff.). In a final exchange in *antilabe*, Pentheus anticipates a triumphal return to Thebes 'in his mother's arms' and the stranger encourages him in ambiguous responses whose real meaning is chillingly clear to all but his victim (955ff.). The stranger has the last word again: he predicts suffering for Pentheus whose fame will 'reach to the sky' (972) and victory for himself and the god.

In an intense fourth stasimon (977-1023), the Chorus invoke madness to strike Pentheus and prophesy the vengeance of their Bacchic sisters against him. Though they speak in the future tense, they simultaneously evoke what is happening to Pentheus at that very moment, as though they have divine power to see beyond events on stage. A hideous revenge on the 'ungodly, unlawful, unjust son of Echion' is considered divine justice (991-6 = 1013-16) and the fifth episode (1024-1152) begins with the news of his death. At this, the Chorus excitedly affirm Dionysus' true divinity, for which they are reproached by the loyal messenger, but their paramount concern is that they are now free from persecution, since Dionysus, not Thebes, commands their loyalty and, in their eyes, Pentheus has met a just end (1031ff.).

Euripides: Bacchae

The messenger reports that when they sat silently watching the Maenads on Cithaeron, this was not enough for Pentheus, who embraced his doom by complaining that he could not see their 'shameful deeds' properly (1048-62.) The stranger obliged him by taking the top of a pine tree and slowly bending it to the ground.[11] Pentheus clambered on and was raised up in the air. His view of the Maenads – and theirs of him – was now fine (1075). And suddenly the stranger had vanished and they heard a voice – the god himself, according to the messenger – which called the women to punish the man who mocked their rites. A line of fire ran from earth to sky. Everything was still. The women stood listening as Dionysus called again (1084-7).

Then they shot forward and threw stones and pine branches at Pentheus, but they could not reach him (1088-1102). And so, with that superhuman strength with which they had once torn bulls apart, they ripped up the roots of the tree as Agave urged them to 'catch the climbing beast'. Down Pentheus fell (1111-12). Agave laid hands on him first and although he tore off his disguise and called on her as his mother, even admitting his mistake (1120-1), she was beyond reason. The god gave her strength to tear her son apart (1128) and she and her fellows played ball with pieces of his flesh until the forest was covered with fragments of Pentheus. In the belief that she and her fellow-hunters had killed a lion cub in a glorious hunt (1129ff.), Agave completed her desecration of her son's body by impaling his head on her thyrsus. The messenger concludes that it is best to be moderate (*sôphronein*) and honour the gods (1137ff.).

The Chorus respond with a brief song, praising Dionysus but acknowledging Pentheus' horrific fate (1153-67), and the *exodos* (1168-1392) begins as Agave arrives, exactly as the messenger had described her. She has not returned to sanity and the Chorus treat her cautiously: they humour her delusion a little (1188, 1192-3) but demur when invited to a victory feast, presumably with the 'lion' as the main dish. Agave happily remembers the hunt and anticipates what her son and the Thebans will say of a triumph accomplished with nothing more than her bare hands (1194ff.).

She calls for her father and Pentheus and demands a ladder so that her quarry's head may be nailed up for all to see. At this, Cadmus arrives with Pentheus, or rather his remains, which he has gathered from Cithaeron and attempted to reassemble (1213-32). She boasts to Cadmus that the normal expectations of women no longer apply to her, now that she has 'left the loom' and won such a prize and invites him to a celebratory dinner. Cadmus responds with grief (*penthos*) and anger towards Dionysus for a revenge which he considers just but excessive (1249-50). Agave judges his response ungenerous and hopes for more enthusiasm from the son for whose future hunting prowess and devotion to Dionysus she prays, even as she holds his head on her thyrsus (12251ff.). When she asks again for Pentheus, Cadmus can take no more. Using a series of questions, he draws her thoughts away from the hunt and towards her marriage to Echion and the baby they had. When she acknowledges Pentheus as her child, Cadmus asks her to look carefully at what she carries (1277), and, although she resists identifying it at first, he persists until she abandons her delusion. The roles of questioner and answerer are now reversed as Agave asks Cadmus what she did on Cithaeron and concludes that Dionysus was to blame (1288-97). At 1300 Agave asks whether Pentheus' body has been reassembled, but our text then breaks off and resumes in the middle of a moving account by Cadmus of his relationship with his only grandson. A slightly more sympathetic Pentheus emerges here: he had been Cadmus' hope for the future and protector in old age, although his protection manifested itself in threats of revenge on anyone who hurt his grandfather (1302-12, 1316-22). Now Cadmus faces vulnerable and lonely exile instead of a glorious old age in Thebes (1313-15, 1323-6).

At 1329 there is another gap, up to 50 lines long, in the text, which resumes in the middle of a speech by Dionysus, appearing finally in his true divine form, perhaps on the *theologeion*, in which he prophesies Cadmus' future. With his wife Harmonia, he will be turned into a snake and lead the barbarians against Greece by command of Zeus' oracle: eventually Ares will grant them life in the land of the blessed.

Dionysus reminds them that his divinity is now vindicated and that their punishment had been entirely avoidable. Cadmus acknowledges that he was wrong but maintains that the punishment was too severe because gods should not equal humans in anger (1348). Dionysus replies that Zeus decreed this long ago.

Cadmus and Agave bid farewell, and lament imminent exile (1352ff.). Agave complains again of Dionysus' cruelty (1374f.). If the text is right, Dionysus (apparently off stage) again asserts the justice of his revenge, but some scholars ascribe the line (with minor alteration) to Cadmus (p. 73 below). Agave prepares for exile with her sisters, and hopes never to encounter Bacchic religion again. As always, the Chorus have the last word: the ways of the gods, exemplified by the events at Thebes, are mysterious.[12]

The two gaps in the text at 1300 and 1329 have occasioned much discussion. A later source asserts that during one of them Agave raised each of Pentheus' limbs and lamented over it, and we can assume that at some point his torn body was reassembled. There is also a definite but unclear relationship between the end of the *Bacchae* and a scene in the *Christus Patiens*, whose twelfth-century author had a complete text of the *Bacchae* which he mined for lines which could express Mary's lamentations over Christ's body.[13] Beyond this, it is impossible to know what happened in the lost portions of the play, but some possibilities are more likely than others. At 1300, when Agave asks, 'Is the body laid together properly?' Cadmus would either have answered, 'No', in which case Agave herself could have reassembled her son's limbs, or something like, 'Yes, but we need his head', which Agave could then set on the corpse. Either way, it seems likely that after she has regained sanity she would not wish to keep her son's head on her thyrsus, and that some restoration of Pentheus' body happened sooner rather than later. At 1329, when the text breaks off after Agave states, 'O father, you see how much my situation has changed', the only remaining business is the burial of Pentheus, and Willink suggests that the line begins a request by Agave for help with the body, followed by Cadmus' response. Perhaps the rest of the gap was filled by Dionysus' vindication of his claims and prophecy of punishments for the unbelievers, in the middle of which our text resumes.[14]

4

Under the Influence

The framework of Euripides' *Bacchae* is highly traditional: a mortal opposes a divinity and is disproportionately punished for his transgression. Moreover, the divinity involved is Dionysus, the patron god of the theatre whose sufferings in popular Greek tradition were often believed to be the original subject of tragedy. The god's vindication of his divinity to unbelievers is a frequent motif of Dionysus myth,[1] and it is plausible that his 'sufferings' might have included the kind of indignities that sceptics like Pentheus attempted to heap on him: motifs similar to those of the *Bacchae* appear in Aeschylus' fragmentary *Edoni* which antedates Euripides' play by at least a half-century, and since the dramatic form of the *Bacchae* recalls earlier tragedy in style, metre, choral songs and in the prominence of the Chorus itself,[2] it is often suggested that this play recalls earlier forms of tragedy. The *Bacchae* also contains elements of a theoxeny, another traditional mythical structure in which a god roams the earth in disguise, rewarding or punishing men according to how they treat him. Yet within this archaising framework lurk highly contemporary conflicts between the rational and the irrational, religion and scepticism, and liberalism and conservatism which are being constantly played out in many different ways and places in the modern world.

'Most terrible and most kind to men' (861)

It is appropriate that Dionysus' play blends contemporary and traditional elements, because Euripides' Dionysus[3] transcends the boundaries between male and female, Greek and non-

50

Greek, god and man, and man and animal which were fundamental to Greek society and particularly male identity (cf.
pp. 12-13 above). In the *Bacchae* Dionysus is 'whatever he
wanted to be' (478). He is unquestionably divine, but because
his mother was a mortal his status remains ambiguous and
vulnerable to human scepticism. Rather than dispelling this
ambiguity with an immediate divine epiphany, he seems to revel
in it and appears for most of the play disguised as a human male
(4, 53-4). From 576-603, he is off stage as a divine voice
exhorting his followers (cf. 1079-88) and only at the very end of
the play is he physically present in his divine form (1329 ff.).
Even the Chorus, who treat the stranger with the reverence due
to a god, never realise that the imagined divine leader of their
rituals (140) really is among them. The stranger maintains a
studied ambiguity, clear to the audience but not to those on
stage, about his relationship with Dionysus by consistently
referring to the god in the third person. At times he comes close
to revealing that he and Dionysus are one and the same. When
an increasingly frustrated Pentheus asks where the god is, he
replies (502), 'Where I am.' Mostly, however, he distances
himself from Dionysus,[4] and even dissociates himself from
phenomena he himself created. When describing Pentheus'
pursuit of a phantom during the earthquake scene (629-30), he
pretends uncertainty as to its origin: 'and then Bromius made,
or so I think – I give you my opinion here – a phantom.' The
mixture of revelation and concealment is typical of his ambiguity throughout the play.

   Although he is disguised as a human male, his appearance is
decidedly feminine and, since he comes from the East (Lydia in
modern-day Turkey), he seems to conform to all the stereotypes
of Eastern effeminacy held by Pentheus and probably by many
members of the audience.[5] His very birth blurred gender: when
his father Zeus[6] blasted his mother Semele with lightning, he
rescued him and set him in his 'male womb' (525-6) so that he
could be born from his father's thigh.[7] And yet, because he is
Semele's son, he is a native Theban male, just like his cousin
Pentheus. A god of such ancestry erodes distinctions between
Greek and barbarian in a manner potentially disturbing to

Greeks whose image of themselves was closely connected with the idea of barbarian inferiority. Dionysus challenges both the notion that Greeks and barbarians should keep separate from one another – his cities mingle them (19) – and the assumption that Greeks are superior to barbarians (483-4). His feminine barbarian appearance and passive behaviour conceal the super-human power which destroys Pentheus. From a logical perspective, he is a new god and so his claims to worship are in doubt, but from the perspective of religious faith, he is Zeus' son and must be properly honoured. The two perspectives are irreconcilable from a purely rational point of view, but one recurring theme of the play is the inadequacy of reason in dealing with Dionysus. Hence those who support Dionysus, such as the Chorus and Tiresias, frequently condemn reliance on intellect (200, 395, 427-32) and instead champion the vaguer concept of ancestral custom (71-2, 201), which softens hard intellectual distinctions and has a broader appeal to the common people.

Except when his own status must be acknowledged, Dionysus is anti-hierarchical. All must participate in his rituals: men and women, Greek and barbarian, old and young (205-6). To devotees, he grants power to transcend their normal abilities. Bacchic religion is physically taxing (135-6) and demands a vigour usually associated with youth and masculinity, and so when he frees women from their confinement indoors, he gives them strength to run in the countryside. The old are given similar power: the old, blind seer Tiresias has been so rejuvenated that, contrary to tragic convention, he does not need an attendant to guide his steps, while at 193 the equally aged Cadmus offers to be his *paedagogus* (literally the slave who led a boy from his home to school and back, often also translated as tutor), as though Tiresias were a child.[8]

Dionysus is god, man and also animal. He can conjure up phantom bulls (618) and appear himself as a bull to the maddened Pentheus (922, cf. 1017-18). The Maenads' fawnskin dress (111, 136, 696-7) is an outward manifestation of the blurring of man and animal in the cult of a being who embraces human, divine and animal form and of the traditional assimilation of women and nature.[9] The Chorus are frequently compared with animals in similes (165-9, 866-76, 1056): at 446, they 'skip', a word often used of young animals.

The natural world can be beautiful and bountiful and Dionysus as a god closely tied to nature offers generous gifts to his adherents. Through his power, the mountain and every creature on it participate in joyous revelry (726-7). He is a god of fecundity who brings an abundance of wine and other liquids fundamental to human well-being out of the ground (107-8, 141, 706-11). The Chorus' description of his worship in the *parodos* is wonderfully sensual: the ground flows with milk, wine and honey while the god waves his fiery torch 'like the smoke of Syrian incense,' as his hair streams in the breeze (142-50).

But Nature is not always benevolent. Just as the Dionysus of cult is associated with life and with death, so Euripides' Dionysus is a god of vigorous fecundity who presides over violent destruction, a combination elegantly symbolised as early as 10-11 in the image of the green vine shoots streaming over his mother's smouldering tomb. This Dionysus both lives in the life of an animal, and also spurs his followers to appropriate that life in *sparagmos*. The *parodos* of the Chorus embraces the loveliness and the horror of his religion: they demand holiness around the 'violent' wands (113) and call *sparagmos* a 'raw-flesh-eating delight' (138), a phrase equally paradoxical in Greek and English. As the son of the lightning god Zeus, Dionysus is often associated with fire (146-7, 596-9, 624, 1083), which is similarly ambiguous in bringing warmth, beauty and purification, but also destruction, as Semele found to her cost (3, 8, 244).

In the ancient world, as in the modern, wine brings relaxation and freedom from cares (280-3, 381-3, 772-4) and at first glance the Dionysus of the *Bacchae* is a figure of liberation:[10] he sends the Theban women out of confinement at home onto the mountains and easily evades capture by Pentheus (443-8, 645-6). And yet he imposes a vicious compulsion on those who refuse to be liberated. As Tiresias recognises in his striking admonition that 'we must be slaves' to him (366, cf. 324), no one is free even to ignore Dionysus, much less resist him. As punishment for Thebes' refusal to acknowledge him, Dionysus has *forced* the Theban women to be Bacchae (33-6), in contrast to the peaceful liberation which the Chorus claim as the god's way. A liberation forced upon the unwilling is paradoxical. Though more associated with (female) emotion and instinct than (male) reason, Dionysus is coldly logical in defending his honour – in the prologue, he is insistent on explaining the reasons for his anger at Thebes – Pentheus scorns him, *because of which* Dionysus must show himself to Thebes as a god (47, cf. 30) *because of which* (53) he has adopted mortal form. Combined with his logic is a steely determination to vindicate his parentage by whatever means are necessary and thus the words *chrê* and *dei,* both meaning 'it is necessary', are frequent in the play.[11]

Dionysus, then, is a complex god and his mixture of benefi-cence and cruelty makes his portrayal in the *Bacchae* problematic. Nature may sometimes seem cruel, but it is essen-tially impersonal – amoral, not immoral. In contrast, Dionysus is so anthropomorphised that it seems impossible to divorce his actions from all moral judgment. To many in the play, he is very attractive: the Chorus, the first servant (434ff.) and the messenger who tells Pentheus that if he had seen the god's miracles he too would worship him (712-13, cf. 769-74) are all converts, as are Cadmus and Tiresias, though their acceptance is more nuanced. Agave and the women of Thebes also worship Dionysus, although through the god's compulsion. Only Pentheus is hostile to Dionysus from the start and regards him as inimical to civilised society. By the end of the play, however, only the Chorus retain their allegiance and of the converts who reappear, Cadmus has lost his enthusiasm and Agave's last wish (1383-6) is never to see the thyrsus again. Thus the destruction of the royal house of Thebes is central to the moral significance of the *Bacchae.* Does Dionysus destroy Pentheus to punish his wilful and impious ignorance in rejecting his cult, so that we must, if reluctantly, accept the justice of his revenge? Or is Pentheus' hostility to Dionysus ultimately vindicated by the god's cruelty? To make any sort of answer to these fundamental questions it is necessary to consider the nature of the cult which Dionysus leads.

The cult

The words of the Chorus and of the messenger (660ff.) offer two perspectives on Dionysiac religion. The Chorus' life centres on their god, and they frequently praise his blessings of the *thiasos*, the dance and relaxation in the wilds (75, 378-85, 417-20, 572-3), all of which are fundamental to their ideals of holiness and to their ideas of true wisdom (71-7, 370ff.). Peace is integral to this wisdom (389-90, cf. 647) as is occasional escapism (403-16; 902-4).[12] The Chorus comprehensively reject normal duties and ambitions in favour of living for the moment with what Dionysus brings: they shun those who strive endlessly for what lies beyond them (428) and commend instead 'thinking like a mortal' (396-9), which for them means concentrating on what is near and whatever ordinary people desire (431-2).[13] Such statements are concentrated in their earlier songs, but a rather different note begins to sound as the play progresses. Dionysus, though a democrat who offers wine to all (421-3), cannot tolerate opposition: he 'hates' (424) those who reject his life and the Chorus follow their master in dividing the world into friends or enemies. For them, Pentheus is an enemy of the true divine (543-4, 988-90), and gradually a kind of fundamentalism emerges in their religion: either one is for Dionysus and saved, or against him and damned. Their third stasimon (862-910) alternates between praising peace and desiring revenge, which they apparently equate with wisdom (see below). Revenge is the dominant theme of the fourth stasimon as they invoke their god to punish the 'godless, unjust' Pentheus (995-7). But even while praying for a sword through their enemy's throat they continue to claim the 'happy life' of wisdom and piety and acting like a mortal.[14] The Chorus, then, reflect Dionysus' combination of peace and violence. The later songs emphasise more openly his violent element, but already the *parodos* mentions 'violent wands' (113) and the bloody hunt (139-40).

The Chorus provide an insider's view of Dionysiac cult. By contrast, the messenger is an outsider and his account is important because he is relatively unbiased: he is a convert because of what he has seen, not through hearsay or prejudice and, because he is Pentheus' man, his plea to his master to accept the god (713-4) is striking. His speech shows unquestionably that the god is real, powerful and worthy of worship, and yet what he describes could make him a witness for the prosecution as much as the defence. At first, his Dionysus is the Chorus' peaceful, generous god. Pentheus' fantasies of orgiastic behaviour are refuted by the description of the worshippers' 'moderation' and 'good order' (686-7, 693): though their thyrsi bring forth wine from the ground (707), they do not abuse it and some even prefer milk or honey (708-11). Peace and harmony abound in their band: they are a unity in diversity, young and old alike (694), all intent on worship. Yet there is something strange about them. They tie their fawnskins with snakes which lick their cheeks and they suckle gazelles or wolf cubs, rather than the children whom they have left behind (697-702). This is a perfect image of the complex relationship of Euripides' Dionysus with the normal life of the Greek city: the women's harmony with the natural world is undoubtedly beautiful, and yet they are also wasting precious milk on an alien species, rather than giving it to the children who will be the soldiers and child-bearers of the next generation of Thebes. Dionysus' religion offers a potentially dangerous mingling of human and animal nature by undermining the traditional hierarchies of Greek society which place men over women and humans over animals. Its danger appears at the end of the play as Agave no longer distinguishes between human and animal in her *sparagmos* on the son whom she sees as a 'climbing beast' (1107-8).[15]

The women enjoy a peaceful cult when left alone, but once men intrude (728, 1062ff.), peace and beauty yield to hideous violence. The men manage to escape but their cattle do not, and the women's rage is uncontrollable. They tear apart with their bare hands whole bulls (745, cf. 1109) – emblems of masculinity – and Dionysus reverses the natural order of the sexes by giving them strength to wound and rout males themselves: the thyrsus trounces the male weapons of iron (764, cf. 736).[16] Euripides dwells graphically on the gory scene as they fling lumps of flesh up and down (741) and the trees drip with blood as the thyrsi had dripped with honey (742; 711). The god's power strikes right at the Greek house. Fresh from their bloody rampage they raid the village like enemies (752), taking children and property from their homes.[17] Equally suddenly and unsettlingly, their rage abates: they return to their streams and the last we see is the snakes licking the blood off their cheeks (760).

The cult has the potential to destabilise the family. It demands that women abandon their homes to dwell briefly with one another in the wilds away from the normal civilising influence of men in a ritual which includes the prospect of perpetrating violence, even in the midst of the peace and joy which Dionysus also brings. The cult is predicated on violence: even by themselves, the women perform *sparagmos* on an ordinary victim in 'raw-flesh-eating delight', but when the normal ritual is disturbed, its violence moves from one legitimate victim onto a host of unsanctioned victims. Even if the Maenads only attack when spied upon, the cult's innate violence makes it an inherently unstable force. The thyrsus produces life-giving liquids (704ff.), but it is also 'an ivy-covered weapon' which wounds (25, 762): while a respectful attitude to the religion represented by the thyrsus may enable dangerous forces to be temporarily subjected to religious purposes, these forces are volatile and may burst forth at any time. The herdsmen deserve punishment for spying on the Maenads but what they get is excessive, just as Dionysus' destruction of the Theban royal house is 'just, but too much', as Cadmus complains (1249). The excessive element of Dionysus is particularly inimical to the ordered life of the city. Dionysus breaks boundaries, but some boundaries are necessary for a society to function successfully: what remains unclear to this day is the distinction between necessary boundaries and those which are merely a product of unquestioned convention.[18]

The portrayal of Pentheus

Dionysus and his religion are complex as nature is complex –
beautiful, peaceful, generous, unpredictable, violent and unre-
strainable: it is as futile for Pentheus to resist such a force as to
resist a tidal wave. Since Dionysus is a god, however, it is not
merely futile but actively impious. Pentheus fails to understand
this because he perceives the stranger merely as a man whose
counterfeit religion is harming his city. One of the outstanding
aspects of the *Bacchae* is the conflict between the two which
runs through the dialogues of the second to fourth episodes.
These demand exploration in the context of Pentheus' role in
his own destruction, and again some central questions arise:
does he deliberately reject a being whose divinity is so obvious
that his punishment is deserved, or is his impiety somehow
tacitly encouraged by a god who does not really desire his repentance but rather the chance to visit him and his house with
violent vengeance?

The Athenians believed that their system of democracy was
superior to all forms of government and this belief frequently
influenced the ways in which they presented Greek myths in
tragedy. No Athenian tragedy is simple propaganda for democracy, but tragedy does contain political comment from the
perspective of fifth-century Athenians living under a democracy. It is not coincidental that a number of tragedies portray
examples of disastrous government by an absolute ruler or
tyrant who was a familiar bogeyman in Athenian political
thought. Typical of tyrants were thought to be reliance on
violence and distrust of the free speech which Athenians considered central to good government.[19] Pentheus exhibits these
characteristics so clearly that the audience is likely, at least at
first, to have found him decidedly unsympathetic. The servant
who brings Dionysus to Pentheus never challenges him directly,
but it is clear from his embarrassment about binding the
stranger and from his amazement at the liberation of the
women (441, 448), that he does not endorse his master's
actions. Both the messenger and the Chorus claim anxiety over
speaking freely to him (668-71; 775-6). Tiresias and the Chorus

both condemn him for relying on mere force and ignoring what is complex, especially in religious matters (310, 1001). Pentheus is called a *theomachos* – one who fights against the gods (45, 325, 1255) – and he is plainly wrong to deny the existence of a god in whose very theatre the audience were sitting. His immediate response to every obstacle is coercion through violence or imprisonment, especially when he has been verbally trounced by Dionysus (513, 653, 809.) He assumes that Tiresias has corrupted Cadmus for his own gain[20] and threatens violence against the old prophet (259, 346ff.). He wishes to imprison the stranger as a prelude to having him stoned to death (355-7, 497, 509-10), imprisons the Theban Bacchae and threatens to enslave the Chorus (514). When maddened by the god, his violence becomes even more extreme as he imagines over-turning Mount Cithaeron itself (949-50). Even at the end of the play, when Euripides manipulates us into feeling some sympathy for him,[21] as Cadmus laments a grandson who was his protector and the hope of his city (1308, 1312), Pentheus' better nature is connected with violence in the memorable image of his stroking his grandfather's cheek while asking whom he should punish (1318-22, cf. 1310).

Like Creon in Sophocles' *Antigone*, Pentheus is particularly insistent that men must dominate women; he is also hostile to non-Greeks (779, 786.) An Eastern stranger who has power over, and gives power to, women is particularly obnoxious to him. His knowledge of the god is based on hearsay (216, 233). He has unilaterally decided that the rites are a mere excuse for drunken sexual excess (218, 222-5, 1060), and he blasphemously refers to Dionysus, 'whoever he is,' a religious formula usually implying the unknowability of divinity (cf. 769) which he misuses to suggest that the god/stranger is a mere nobody (220, cf. 247). Cadmus, the two messengers and Tiresias all offer him direct warnings against what he is doing. It is axiomatic in tragedy that Tiresias is never wrong, and Euripides retains this convention even though his Tiresias is unconventional in some respects (below, p. 71).

Pentheus' impiety is connected with a lack of intellectual curiosity (490). Because he sees the stranger only as an effeminate peddler of an immoral, barbarian cult, he will not regard miracles such as the liberation of the imprisoned women and the earthquake as manifestations of divine power. Others understand the truth (448, 764, 1069), but Pentheus has no response to Dionysiac miracles except violence and incarceration (653). The stranger's powers in the earthquake scene are particularly spectacular as he wields his father's lightning around his mother's tomb and damages Pentheus' palace. His effortless control contrasts with Pentheus' sweaty attempts to get the better of the divine manifestations of the bull, the fire and the phantom which exhausts him as he stabs it repeatedly (618-34) while the god sits watching him placidly.[22] In Greek thought, the gods do everything easily (cf. 614), and this whole scene proves that Dionysus is truly divine: indeed, he comes close to revealing his identity to the Chorus at 614 by asserting that he saved himself, after having prophesied (498) that the god would save him whenever he wanted. To Pentheus, who has not heard his speech to the Chorus or seen him watching his desperate efforts, he is less forthcoming (649): 'Didn't I tell you that someone would save me?'.

But for a modern audience Pentheus' most immediate characteristic is likely to be, not his behaviour as a politician, but his interest in the supposed sexual activities of the Maenads. His threats of violence alternate with his fascination with seeing them at their business and it is often suggested that his violence stems from an attraction which he dare not admit to himself. His feelings towards the stranger are particularly ambivalent: his description of his sweet-smelling golden hair and rosy but pale, unmasculine complexion, 'full of desire' (236, 438, 455-6), is more than a purely factual description for those of the audience sitting too far back to see him clearly![23] Indeed, he even says (453-4) that Dionysus is 'not unattractive', immediately adding 'for women'. Dionysus' flowing, uncontrolled hair is his particular target (239, 493), perhaps because it symbolises everything that attracts and appalls him. Sexual irregularity was another stereotypical tyrannical trait (Herodotus 3.80.6), but Euripides' portrayal of this aspect of Pentheus seems astonishingly modern to a contemporary audience familiar with terms such as repression or voyeurism.[24] It should be stressed, however, that although modern audiences might condemn Pentheus for his supposedly repressed attraction to Dionysus, for an ancient audience, the violence, impiety and arrogance typical of the tyrants who are destroyed in tragedy would have been far more important reasons for judging him harshly.

Pentheus' failings are those which traditionally attract divine vengeance. Yet Euripides offers him mitigating characteristics as well. Alone among the characters in the play, Pentheus is young (214, 330, 332), and his behaviour could therefore also be understood to reflect the excess of enthusiasm combined with undeveloped judgement that was typical of young people in Greek eyes. He wishes to do his best for the city, but his inexperience leads to an authoritarianism that can endure no challenges, especially not those which Dionysus brings. Since he sincerely believes that Dionysus' cult is bad for Thebes, he tries to suppress it, and although his fate indicates that he was wrong to do so, certain reasons for his disapproval might have struck a chord with his audience. His apparent obsession with sexual irregularities at the rites (222-5, 261-2, 354, 486) might equally be interpreted as concern for the well-being of the women of his city. Those with better knowledge of the cult repeatedly deny such goings-on, but the combination of a night festival and wine was commonly believed to be a recipe for female licentiousness: the new cults introduced at Athens throughout the fifth century were often suspected of exactly the immorality of which Pentheus accuses Dionysus' cult.[25] Euripides even teases us with the possibility that Pentheus might be right by explicitly linking Dionysus with Aphrodite (313-4, 403, 773-4). 'Women's liberation' has very different connotations for modern and ancient audiences, for whom, to judge from frequent references in tragedy and comedy, it was highly unsettling.[26] Thebes is disrupted by the departure of its women to the mountains and Pentheus' suspicion that Dionysus' empowerment of women is not necessarily beneficial is at least partially vindicated when we see Agave holding the thyrsus with her son's head impaled upon it and claiming that she has found victory in 'leaving the loom' for better things (1236-7).[27] The Chorus' immediate reaction to Pentheus' death (1031) might also justify his unease at what the cult can do to its adherents: 'O lord Bromius, you appear as a great god'. To the messenger's expression of shock that this unfeeling response is not 'noble', they assert that not Thebes but Dionysus is their master (1036-7), and they view Pentheus' death at first without compassion. Pentheus' idea of the cult is tragically mistaken in one sense, but it is hard to lay aside all sense that Bacchic worship in some circumstances is inimical to the city. Interestingly, Dionysus-inspired female solidarity against male interests occurs in an anecdote by Plutarch (*Moralia* 249e-f) in which, in a time of war between Phocis and Thebes, some exhausted female worshippers of Dionysus arrived at Amphissa, then allied with Phocis, and fell asleep in the market-place. The women of Amphissa banded together to protect them from being harmed by the Phocian soldiers while they slept.

From Dionysus' perspective, since he is a god, Pentheus' misgivings are simply wrong. Not so simple, however, are the measures he takes against him. Greek gods rarely offer unambiguous information and help to mortals, and Euripides leaves tantalisingly unclear what the god really wants of Pentheus: has he planned his destruction from the start, or are the warnings he gives him through the first two-thirds of the play a genuine attempt to save him from himself? As Tiresias notes, the god is a prophet (498), and the very fact that his control over events is so complete that everything he prophesies happens ought in itself to convince Pentheus that his cult is real. And yet, while he communicates with Pentheus clearly through what he does, what he says to him is often so ambiguous between warning and mockery that it alienates the already sceptical king even further. When Dionysus explains that he cannot tell Pentheus the secrets of initiates (474), but that they are worth hearing, Pentheus accuses him of trying to trap him with intriguing words (475). Is he right or is Dionysus actually attempting to encourage him to join the cult by stimulating his curiosity? Since Dionysus replies that the god hates impiety (476), it would certainly be possible to interpret 474 as a genuine attempt to lead Pentheus away from disaster. The earthquake scene and the messenger's account of his encounter with the Maenads are also clear warnings to Pentheus, but Dionysus' apparent pleasure in his humiliation (616, 632, 635-6, 1081) is unattractive and counter-productive: that a god can beat a mortal is unsurprising and Pentheus is even less amenable to accepting Dionysus after his experiences. When Pentheus threatens to build a wall around the city, Dionysus points out that gods can jump over walls (654). Again, the comment is poised between warning and mockery, yet his advice just before this to be calm (*hêsuchazein*) certainly does not seem mocking (647, cf. 787-90). At 802, Dionysus offers to lead the women to Pentheus without weapons, but the spirit of this is unclear: is it Pentheus' last chance or Dionysus' final confirmation that he deserves to die?[28]

There are no simple answers to some central questions arising from the play, but what is striking is how much in common the two cousins have. Each values his own honour – as Tiresias notes when encouraging Pentheus to worship Dionysus (319) – and seeks to humiliate his rival.[29] Both claim absolute rightness. Pentheus encourages the messenger to speak freely (673) because 'one should not be angry with those who are just': Dionysus would scarcely disagree. Except perhaps in his final scene, Pentheus believes that he is a match for the stranger and even unconsciously emulates him when he threatens to fling Tiresias' seat at Delphi 'upside down' (349), a phrase otherwise associated with Dionysiac confusion (603, 741, 753), and wants to punish the stranger for disrespect just as Dionysus wants to punish him (489-90). Both are vindictive, but whereas Pentheus lacks the intellect to see the stranger for who he must be, Dionysus knows exactly who Pentheus is, and conquers him through this knowledge. The characteristics which Dionysus and Pentheus share ultimately emphasise that there is an unbridgeable gap between gods and men. Cadmus' protest that gods should not resemble men in anger (1348) is an age-old complaint: as far back as Homer, the Greek gods both resemble humans in their desires and differ from us in their power to achieve those desires and in their indifference to pity. Pentheus must command some sympathy because it is so hard to handle the danger and complexity of a force like Dionysus. Conversely, since Dionysus' claims to divinity are unquestionable, his rage at Pentheus' disrespect must be justifiable, but through his very divinity he lacks the humanity which could forgive Pentheus' immaturity and because he is more directly involved in murder than is usual for tragic gods, his vengeance inevitably seems excessive, especially given his disguise and warnings which are clearer to the audience than they are to Pentheus. The combination of the two cousins proves deadly: the tragedy could not have been sparked by a humbler and more intelligent Pentheus meeting the god or a more merciful Dionysus meeting Pentheus.

The battle between Dionysus and Pentheus

Verbal conflict is essential to all Greek tragedy, but the *Bacchae* contains an exceptionally protracted conflict between the two cousins, which builds to a climax through long passages of *stichomythia* in the three central episodes. Through their verbal battles we see a complete reversal of positions from Pentheus' apparent dominance to Dionysus' final triumph, but even when Pentheus seems most dominant over Dionysus, Euripides' dialogue reveals the flimsiness of his power. Though he blusters and threatens the stranger, it is clear that he is unsettled by his ambiguous appearance and by the ambiguous appeal of the cult itself. He tries to take control by aggressively asking question after question of the stranger (460-508), who responds calmly each time so that Pentheus cannot best him. This god of the irrational is unbeatable in verbal combat and throws Pentheus off-balance repeatedly. As the pair vie for dominance by twisting each other's words and flinging them back at one another, Dionysus returns all of Pentheus' seemingly unplayable shots. When Pentheus asks Dionysus what the god looked like and is told 'whatever he wanted', he ineffectively exclaims that he has been sidetracked (479). To Pentheus' threat that Dionysus must 'pay for' his evil tricks (489) comes the response (490), 'And you for your ignorance and impiety'. Pentheus can only respond feebly by complaining of the stranger's boldness (491) and at once Dionysus seizes control: 'What terrible thing will you do to me?' Thus he leads Pentheus into the unwitting utterance of impiety directly against the god's person as he threatens to cut off his hair. The stranger forbids such a direct violation – his hair is 'for the god' – but is otherwise accommodating: he invites Pentheus to take his thyrsus and is unconcerned about imprisonment since (498) 'The god will free me whenever I want'. Pentheus' own lack of curiosity also hinders him. When Dionysus says that the god is 'where I am' (502), he does not enquire further, but commands his men to seize him and ignores the serious warning which Dionysus offers (504-8).

Dionysus' display of his powers in the earthquake scene meets with equal incomprehension. To ignore this direct indication of his power is arguably more culpable than Pentheus' refusal to heed verbal warning from someone he assumes is merely a human being. For him, the conflict is just an issue of Greek male honour (779, 786) and what happens in the palace is simply a military failure which can be remedied by more confinement and military action (653, 792ff., 780-6). Again, they take up each other's words: Dionysus says that he would sacrifice (*thuoimi*) rather than angrily (*thumoumenos*) fight the god as a mortal (794-5), and Pentheus flings his words back at him: I will sacrifice (*thusô*) female blood on Cithaeron (796-7). Dionysus had turned his opponent's violence back on himself in the palace by exhausting him with phantoms. Now he points out that a second rout would be 'shameful', using Pentheus' obsession with dominance to test him further. Pentheus is frustrated at this stalemate (800-1, cf. 491) and through his rival's frustration and longing to encounter the Maenads, Dionysus destroys him.

For nearly 40 lines, Pentheus veers between self-assertion and submission to the god who, through a knowledge of Pentheus which seems deeper than Pentheus' own self-knowledge, cajoles and threatens until his victim is totally his. When Pentheus eagerly accepts his offer to lead him to the Maenads (812), he pretends surprise. Pentheus still has enough self-control to backtrack: of course, it would be 'painful' (814) to see them drunk, but when Dionysus asks why he wishes to see something painful, he cannot explain. The god's influence seems to have made him more suggestible. He immediately agrees that he should visit the Maenads openly (818) and accepts Dionysus' initial instruction to wear women's clothing, even – for the first time – commending his wisdom (824).[30] When the full horror of this sinks in, and he expresses embarrassment at the god's proposal, Dionysus simply shrugs like a haggler in a market (829) and at once Pentheus requests more details of what he must wear (830-5). To his next objection, Dionysus warns that violence will ensue if he does not: he submits (836-7). To the last, however, Pentheus mistakenly believes that he is still in control, by claiming that he has choices, both between wearing women's costume or being bested by the Bacchae and between an armed attack or Dionysus' embarrassing plan (845-6, cf. 843).

Pentheus' last words in this scene are wonderfully ambiguous. *Toisi soisi peisomai bouleumasin* (846) could either mean 'I will obey your plans' or 'I will suffer by means of your plans', and, especially in their last scene together, Euripides uses a remarkable number of double entendres to show Dionysus' mastery over his victim.[31] Throughout the play, the god had made asides to the audience after Pentheus' departures (515-19, 657-61, 847-61) but now he addresses them directly in his victim's presence: by contrast, Pentheus' double entendres are entirely unwitting. Dionysus assures him that the god is 'with him' and he sees 'as he ought' (923). He praises him for having changed his mind, but the Greek word for 'changed' could also mean 'gone out of' (*methestêkas*, 944, cf. 850). Pentheus embraces his doom, by practising diligently as a Bacchante and asking Dionysus to 'adorn' him since he is 'dedicated' to him (934): his unconscious use of sacrificial terminology is all too appropriate since he is the sacrifice that ensures Dionysus' honour in Thebes.[32] Pentheus refused to understand the deeper meaning of the stranger's hints at his identity: now he cannot understand his hints of what will happen (960). He even demands to be carried through Thebes (961) for his unique daring: Dionysus ironically agrees that he is indeed unique and promises that 'the struggles which are proper' are coming his way (964). The final *antilabe* takes double entendre to hideous extremes as the god prophesies his return 'in his mother's arms'. Pentheus, in misguided pride, replies, 'You'll ruin me!'[33] and proclaims that he is getting (970) 'what I deserve'. In a final ironic aside, Dionysus promises him sky-high fame (972).

The death of Pentheus

The desires which motivate Pentheus to go to the mountain cause his death. All Dionysus does is help him when he wishes to see the Maenads' (non-existent) shameful deeds (1062) more clearly, by bending down the top of a pine tree. For the messenger who reports it, this is clearly 'no mortal act' (1069), but Pentheus is long beyond such recognition and climbs 'sky-high' (1073), fulfilling the prophecy of 972. Euripides draws the suspense out to a remarkable degree. At first the Maenads are unaware of Pentheus' presence. Only when a voice ('as one might guess, Dionysus', 1078) calls to them, not once, but, after a pause,[34] twice (1079-81, 1088) are they aware of the interloper. Even then, they cannot reach him with their sticks and stones and so with the 'ironless crowbars' which have already served them well (1104, cf. 736), the women tear up the tree and capture their victim. As 'priestess of the slaughter' (1114), Agave leads the *sparagmos* of the son whom she sees as a 'climbing beast' through her Dionysiac haze (1107-8.) Pentheus cannot convey his identity to his mother: she did not think 'as she ought' because the god himself gave her strength to tear her son apart (1124-8). This scene is even more shocking than that of the previous *sparagmos*: no herd of cows but a human being whom we have known is dismembered and tossed around by Agave and her fellows in a ghastly mingling of the playful and horrific aspects of Dionysus' cult (1136). The contrast between

Pentheus' vulnerability and Dionysus' disregard for human suffering makes the messenger's account of his death particularly horrific. Dionysus sets him on the tree, Dionysus draws the attention of the Bacchae to him and Dionysus gives them the strength to tear him apart. Agave is merely his instrument in Pentheus' murder.

Through the agency of the god who turns everything upside down, everything Agave says after the murder is the opposite of the truth. She is triumphant because Dionysus is the ally (1146-7) who has helped her to kill a lion[35] whose head she strokes maternally (1185-7) on the end of her thyrsus. She seeks admiration from the Chorus and her father for a successful hunt accomplished with none of the weapons which men normally need (1193, 1205-8, cf. 1233-40). Her exultation is expressed in words used earlier to describe the benefits of the Dionysiac life (1006-7,1171, 1180, 1184, 1198, 1242). By contrast, Dionysus' followers in the Chorus are ambivalent about what she has done and this too is expressed in language earlier associated with Dionysus. At 429 they had condemned the *perissoi*, those whose excessive ambitions lead them away from Dionysiac wisdom, but by 1196 they call Agave's hunt *perissan*. They greet the messenger's speech with a short hymn praising Dionysus but they admit that Agave's victory 'ends in tears' (1161-4, cf. 1147). They are also wary of her: they humour her in her delusion and praise her (1193, 1200), but when she offers them a share in the feast they recoil (1184). Although they are pleased at Pentheus' punishment (1041-2), they seem unsettled by what has happened and even eventually express sympathy for Cadmus (1327-8).

Even ordinary Dionysiac ecstasy is only temporary, and Agave's illusory joy finally becomes unsustainable when, as she holds his head in her hands, she asks for Pentheus to come and hang the skull of her prize on the house wall.[36] Her father's gentle questioning draws her away from Dionysiac illusion to sadder human reality. The Dionysiac world is more comfortable: only when Cadmus insists that she look carefully at what she holds does she relinquish the comforting belief that it is an animal's head (1277-81).[37]

4. Under the Influence

The end of the play is its least appealing part to modern readers, especially because of the lacuna between 1329 and 1330 which moves us straight from Agave's lament into the middle of Dionysus' speech: after the gripping conflict between Pentheus and Dionysus, the magical transformation of Cadmus and Harmonia into snakes is jarring. A move from Greece's past to its present is common as a tragedy approaches its end and the audience is being prepared to return to reality: the prophecy that Cadmus and Harmonia will lead barbarians against Thebes (1333-8, 1354-62) and sack many cities until they stop at Delphi, may refer to oracles which predicted an invasion by Easterners during the Persian wars.[38]

What is wisdom (877)?

The enthralling contest between god and man is arguably the play's most immediate attraction, but of equal importance are the philosophical and theological questions embedded in it. At 877, the Chorus ask, 'What is wisdom?' and a series of verbal plays on *sophia* and its cognates explores this question, although the definition of true wisdom is left carefully unclear.[39] It is obviously wise to worship Dionysus: Tiresias is wise, as is Cadmus in following him (179, 186, 196). They agree: 'We do not get rationalistic (*sophizomestha*) concerning the gods, since no logical thought (*logos*) will overthrow the ancestral customs as old as time, not even if the cleverest minds discover what is *sophon*' (201-3). *Sophon* here seems to denote a mere cleverness that excludes the irrational side of life which is integral to Dionysus: true wisdom transcends simple rationalism and encompasses acceptance of Dionysus. The Chorus make a similar distinction when they claim in the first stasimon, 'cleverness is not wisdom' *(to sophon ou sophia,* 395*)*, which they equate with 'thinking like a mortal' (396) and a life of peace and humble ambition: Dionysus himself commends such behaviour to Pentheus (647, cf. 877-90). This stasimon distinguishes between the cleverness of intellectuals and the true wisdom of Dionysus' worshippers. Since Pentheus condemns the cult on intellectual as well as moral grounds (341, cf. 252) and asserts that the barbarians worship Dionysus because they are the Greeks' intellectual inferiors (483), he is one who has *sophon* but not true wisdom. At 655-6, enraged by Dionysus' brilliance in verbal argument, Pentheus himself tries to condemn him as *sophos* merely in the sense of being clever, but by 824 he is under the god's spell and calls him *sophos* with no irony or sarcasm.

However, two major difficulties make uncritical endorsement of Dionysiac wisdom difficult. The first is that a life based on the Chorus' recommendations is, in its refusal of reason and anything beyond the challenges of a daily existence, not much more than an animal's life.[40] Second is the implication that this wisdom sanctions violent revenge. At 877, the transmitted text makes the Chorus ask, 'What is wisdom (*to sophon*)? And what is lovelier as a gift of the gods than to have a hand stronger than one's enemy? What is beautiful is always dear.' An alternative minor adjustment to the punctuation of the text would make it read, 'What is wisdom? Or what is the finer gift from the gods among mortals? Is it to hold a hand over your enemy's head? [No, for] what is fine is dear always.'[41] But given the Chorus' enthusiasm for revenge at 992f. and the context of this statement, so soon after Dionysus has revealed the humiliation which awaits Pentheus, I think, with many commentators, that these words must indicate that violent revenge is fundamental to Dionysiac religion.

The Chorus' devoted and literal belief contrasts with Tiresias' faith, which he expresses in complex arguments that have stylistic and thematic connections with the philosophical speculations of some of Euripides' contemporaries.[42] This is ironic given the consistent condemnation of excessive intellectualism by Dionysus' supporters (including Tiresias himself at 200f.) elsewhere in the play. Moreover, his scene with Cadmus apparently injects humour into the middle of a tragedy and this too makes any interpretation of what he says about Dionysus difficult.[43] Nonetheless, though superficially novel, his view is orthodox in acknowledging that Dionysus is never contained by normal boundaries. Tiresias' Dionysus has powers traditionally associated with other gods: he is like Apollo[44] in giving people the power to prophesy, and he shares with Ares a power over armies, his feminine appearance notwithstanding (302). Even more importantly, he prophesies that the new god '*will* be' great in Greece (274), but simultaneously ranks him with the ancient giver of corn Demeter, as god of the equally venerable substance of wine (275-83),[45] making Dionysus old and new at once – an impossibility for those bound by the logic of the false *sophon*.[46] Whereas the Chorus believe that Dionysus was literally born from Zeus' thigh, Tiresias ingeniously explains the miracle through mistaken etymology: Dionysus was not sewn in the thigh (*ho mêros*) of Zeus but was Hera's hostage (*homeros*). That his explanation depends so heavily on the logic which he earlier condemned is paradoxical and the explanation seems actually to detract from something of Dionysus' divine mystery; yet he never denies that Dionysus is Zeus' son, so preserves the fundamental theological framework of the story and some of Dionysus' innate character.

Tiresias' interpretation is therefore novel but respectful. By contrast, Pentheus cannot abandon the distinctions between the roles of men and women or Greeks and barbarians rooted in the conventional wisdom whose opposite is the Dionysiac wisdom which necessitates acceptance of a 'madness' that brings ecstasy and the negation of everyday perception. For Dionysus, Pentheus' rigid refusal to accept him means that he is not only stupid (480) but already mad, and his perception is 'sick' (311-12, 326, 332, 359). He sends him mad to prove that worshipping him is wise. For Dionysus, you are mad if you are too sane (in Pentheus' definition) to submit to him: compulsory madness is the only sanity. At 641, Dionysus commends *sôphrosynê* as a part of *sophia*. The word literally means 'safe-mindedness' and includes good sense and self-control. *Sôphrosynê*, like logical argument, would hardly seem Dionysiac, but Dionysus controls even the language in the play so that the god of madness and his Bacchae have *sôphrosynê* but Pentheus does not (504, 940.) The messenger understands Pentheus' end as a sign that to have *sôphrosynê* (*sôphronein*) and honour the gods is the wisest (*sophôtaton*) action for humans (1150) and Dionysus agrees (1341): *sôphrosynê*, equated with worshipping him, would have saved Thebes. In itself, mingled madness and sanity could be the benign escapism that the Chorus associates with the god, just as Dionysiac ritual can be beneficial if performed without interruption. Indeed, both Tiresias and Dionysus claim that Dionysus transcends morality and that his effect on an individual depends on the individual's character: even in the midst of revelry, the truly *sôphron* will not come to moral harm (317-18, 488). Pentheus' fate seems to prove this point. And yet, at least for Agave, it is not so simple: Dionysus deliberately sends her mad so that her normal perception is corrupted rather than merely altered as she becomes his instrument of revenge on Pentheus. Moreover, the exaltation that he brings is by definition temporary but its effects can be disastrously eternal, as Cadmus sees when lamenting the cruel necessity of bringing his daughter back to normality and the knowledge of what she has done (1259-62).

Cadmus

Unlike his grandson, Cadmus survives, but in a woefully diminished state. He is ostensibly a believer in Dionysus and yet his belief seems ambivalent. Although he urges unstinting worship of the god (181-2) and Dionysus himself praises him for having sanctified the place at which Semele was blasted (10), his enthusiasm is qualified: though he questions Tiresias on techniques of Bacchic dancing and claims that he could never grow tired of it (184-8), he also suggests (191) that they ride, rather than walk, to Cithaeron. Since Bacchic worship demands the physical effort which brings total surrender to the god and Tiresias dismisses his suggestion as offering insufficient honour to Dionysus (192), it begins to look as though he is withholding something. It is hard not to suspect that Dionysus' most important attribute for Cadmus is the glory which his birth to Semele sheds on the royal house of Thebes. At 181, he adds his own connection with Dionysus as 'my daughter's son' to his command to worship him even while entertaining the possibility that Dionysus might not be genuinely divine (332-6): 'Even if he is not a god, as you say, then let him be called one by you so that Semele may seem to have given birth to a god and honour may attend the whole family.' Even if his words are merely an attempt to placate Pentheus, this is not the unquestioning respect which the god demands. Perhaps Cadmus is punished so severely because his worship was in the end half-hearted:[47] there is an exquisite irony in Dionysus' eventual destruction of the house of a man so concerned with family honour. Cadmus distances himself from his daughters' mistakes ('You denied Dionysus', 1297, 1304) and complains of his harsh treatment: his statement that the god 'justly, but excessively destroyed us [though] he was of our house' (1249-50, cf. 1304), suggests that he finds his conduct treacherous. At 1344 he takes equal blame for their wrong-doing, but at 1346 he complains that the god was excessive and at 1348 that gods should not resemble men in anger.[48] He has still not fully understood a god unmoved by the human relationships so central to him. For Dionysus, the recognition of his divinity trumps all human concerns and he answers Cadmus' complaints simply: my father Zeus decreed long ago that this should happen. This is both a simple acknowledgement that life is unfair, and a final assertion of his bond with Zeus: whether Cadmus considers this a valid explanation is largely irrelevant to Dionysus. A textual uncertainty leaves Cadmus' final judgment unclear, however: the transmitted text of 1377 reads '*epaschon deina pros humon*' ('I suffered terribly from you') and must be assigned to Dionysus, who has not spoken since 1351. Commentators who find such a long silence unlikely suggest that *epaschon* should read *epaschen* ('*he* suffered terribly') and attribute the line to Cadmus, who would therefore seem a little more sympathetic to the god's claims than the transmitted text suggests.[49]

Language and structure

Euripides conveys the major themes of his text through a multitude of parallels and echoes in words and actions. Tiresias calls the newly-dressed Cadmus out of the house just as Dionysus summons the newly-dressed Pentheus to meet the Bacchae (170; 912). Pentheus comes on stage in answer to alarming news that he has heard, just as Cadmus does (216; 1222). Pentheus threatens to cut off Dionysus' head: his own head will be impaled on his mother's thyrsus (241; 1141). Pentheus threatens the god with stoning and will be stoned by the Maenads (356; 1096). Dionysus' feminine good looks contrast with Pentheus' implied masculinity, but by 912 Pentheus is attired in fawnskin, thyrsus, long hair and a *peplos*,[50] and, though Pentheus condemns him as 'female-like' (*thêlymorphon*, 353), Dionysus prophesies that Pentheus will be led 'woman-like' (*gunaikomorphon*, 855, cf. *gunaikomimôi*, 980) through the city. At 492ff. Pentheus threatens to destroy Dionysus' costume, but by 830 he is asking the god's advice on his own costume. Pentheus longs to see the Maenads, but at 1075 'he was seen, rather than saw'.

The hunt is central to Dionysiac cult (135-40) and hunting-imagery is especially important in expressing the exchange of power between Dionysus and Pentheus.[51] At first, Dionysus and his band are the prey of Pentheus and his minions (228, 353, 434-6, 719, 732), but by 865ff. the Chorus compare themselves with a fawn who has escaped the hunter, and soon Agave hunts her son down like an animal and boasts of her success with her fellow hunter Dionysus (1107-8, 1146, 1171, 1183, 1188-9, 1192). Pentheus' death is foreshadowed by that of his cousin Actaeon at his own hounds' teeth for unwise self-assertion over Artemis (337). Actaeon's hounds were female and, like the Bacchae, they are 'raw-flesh-eating' (338), just as at 731 the Bacchae are called 'hunting dogs'. Above all, the action and language of the first hunt foreshadow Agave's hunt for Pentheus. In both, the peaceful business of the Maenads is disturbed by a male intrusion which is punished by destruction at 'countless' (*murios*, 745, 1109) female hands. Blood is every-where (742, 1135) as they rip apart (739, 746, 1210) the limbs in the *sparagmos* (735, 739, 1104, 1135). Pentheus wondered if he could prize up Cithaeron with his crowbar (949), but his tree is uprooted by the women's 'ironless' crowbars (1104, cf. 736).

Three other words are notable for the way their shifts in

meaning over the course of the play follow the shifting of the balance of power between Dionysus and Pentheus. The word *deinos* denotes anything out of the ordinary, whether amazing or terrible, and Euripides plays on its multiple meanings. The messenger is a convert to Dionysus because of the *deina* actions of the Bacchae (667, 716). Pentheus uncomprehendingly interprets his word in its other sense, reassuring him that the more *terrible* things he says about the Bacchae the more he can punish those who corrupted them (674, cf. 760). The use of *deinos* also underlines the theme of reversal: Pentheus was *deinos* (terrible) at first to Dionysus (492, 856), but becomes *deinos* (strange), the victim of *deina* (strange and terrible) sufferings (971). Dionysus answers Agave's complaint at his terrible revenge with an appeal to the terrible (*deina*) dishonour he suffered (1374, 1377).

The words *dei* and *chrê* generally refer to what is 'necessary', what 'ought' to happen (789, 912), but in this play they are especially connected with the worship that Dionysus 'ought' to have but is not receiving. His aunts 'who least ought to have done' (26) have denied him and so the city 'ought' to learn who he is and join in his rites (39, cf. 181, 207). At 1345 he reiterates that the Thebans did not learn when they 'ought' to have done. The two words also refer to his knowledge of fate, what 'ought' to happen: the god of spontaneity is fixedly in control. He is confident that Pentheus' threats will come to nothing since 'one must not suffer what must not happen' (515-6). To Pentheus' complaint that he is 'so clever, except where you ought to be', he calmly responds, 'I am clever exactly where I ought to be' (656). The two meanings are connected: Pentheus *must* die because Dionysus *must* be honoured. Pentheus is eager to see what (if he had the right attitude) he ought not to see (912-3) but, since he must be punished, when he sees Dionysus no longer as a human but as a bull, the god commends him for thinking 'as you ought' (924, cf. 948), now that he is compliant in his fate. After this, the words acquire extra menace by shifting slightly in meaning from 'what ought to happen' to 'what you deserve'. At 955, Dionysus tells Pentheus, 'You will be hidden as you ought/deserve to be hidden'; at 964, 'The struggles which ought to, await you.' But in the messenger's mouth, the earlier meaning of the word, without connection with Dionysus, returns and underlines the horror of what he has made Agave do: she kills her son because she did *not* think as she ought (1123).

Metaphor and metatheatre[52]

Yet another dimension is added to the play by Euripides' manipulation of metaphor and theatrical convention. The god who alters perception also presides over the movement of metaphor into reality and vice versa. Pentheus' name derives from the Greek for 'grief' (*penthos*) and the man of grief comes to grief (367-8, 508, cf. 1244). Tiresias says that Pentheus does not know where he is in his words (358), an opinion which Dionysus states even more strongly (506), and the metaphor becomes literal in the fourth episode, in which Pentheus truly does not know what he is doing. Conversely, literal acts are symbolic. The destruction of Pentheus' palace foreshadows that of his family[53] and Pentheus' helplessness against a greater power is encapsulated in the image of his attempts to fight phantoms as the stranger watches quietly (622). The dualities that run through the play are outwardly manifested in the presence of the Chorus whose physical presence invokes the Theban Bacchae off stage, especially in the frenetic fourth stasimon (977-1023), where they invoke the scene on Cithaeron. Even the play's emphasis on Bacchic costume may symbolise a literal truth. Both Cadmus and Pentheus are concerned to look like proper worshippers (181ff., 930-44), but, under their fawnskins, certainly Pentheus and arguably Cadmus are not true devotees.

All we have of the original production of the *Bacchae* is an incomplete text: as readers we can only imagine the Chorus' costumes and hear their musical instruments (513-4, cf. 58-61, 128, 156, 160). The characters of the play themselves make unusually frequent references to the equipment of Dionysiac worship (176-7, 249-51, 341, 363, 830-5 and especially 912ff.) and to the theatre and theatrical practices. Dionysus calls Pentheus an eager spectator (*theatês*) of the Maenads (829), just as the audience are spectators of his fate. When, as he rehearses his role as Bacchante, Pentheus asks if he resembles his mother (926), the question is ironic in the context of the theatrical convention according to which the same actor would play Pentheus in this scene and Agave in the *exodos*.[54] Euripides also draws attention to the stranger's smiling mask: he kept smiling as he was arrested (438-9) and the Chorus ask him to come 'with smiling face' to capture Pentheus (1021).[55] Dionysus is the god of both tragedy and comedy and the god who blurs boundaries: although the *Bacchae* is a tragedy, not only does it contain some comic moments, such as the sight of the two old buffers decked out in fawnskins ('a big laugh' according to Pentheus, 250), but also some dramatic techniques which are standard in comedy; notably, the double entendre-filled asides to the audience and byplay with costumes.[56] Even the excessiveness of Dionysus' revenge may have some metatheatrical significance. All the Greek divinities tend towards excess: in tragedy, they mete out punishments which do not merely match the offence but are far in excess of it. Naturally tragedy's patron provides an exceptionally ghastly punishment for the one who transgresses against him.

Dionysus: god or something other?

All who come under his spell agree with Dionysus that true wisdom consists in honouring him (1341-3, cf. 329, 1150-2, 1325) and, yet, his revenge is so pitiless that this conclusion seems inadequate, especially given Agave's rejection of Bacchic religion. Which takes precedence? Revulsion and rejection of Dionysus? Condemnation of Pentheus and a concomitant devotion to the god? A grudging worship based on fear? Surely not this: conversion through fear or opportunism is no conversion. Dionysus' blessings are real and his revenges are cruel. To receive his blessings demands wholehearted belief like that of the Chorus and the courage to accept the whole god. Dionysiac worship is essential but his innate character makes it complex: to worship him is to accept that which lies beyond the normal boundaries of human society. The god renders unstable and

uncertain the world of conventional wisdom and normal perception, where men are men, and women are women. The tragedy
of the *Bacchae* is that Pentheus will not grasp this and
Dionysus will not show him mercy for his inability to grasp
what is so difficult.

Greek theology conceptualises the gods as beings who
preside over certain elements of existence which themselves can
take the god's name: Aphrodite is the goddess of love and sex,
and so love and sex can be 'Aphrodite'. Through this flexible
idea of divinity, where personified divinity and what the divinity
represents are neither synonymous nor entirely distinct,
Euripides' Dionysus transcends even his main incarnation as
an anthropomorphised divinity. He is his own gift of wine – 'a
god, he is poured out to the gods' (284) – and by extension he is
also the experiences that wine offers. Thus Dionysus is person
and drink and experience: different conceptualisations will
generate different versions of the play. If Dionysus is seen as a
god, the play concerns one man's impious striving against a
superior power, but a more symbolically imagined Dionysus
generates other interpretations of the play in which he represents a power that removes people from normality, for good or
ill.[57] To give an obvious example, wine brings sleep and forgetfulness of troubles (280-3, 381-3), but in excess it is harmful.
Pentheus actually appears drunk in his last scene with
Dionysus: he sees double, he is aggressive and even his scrupu-
lous imitation of Bacchic movements resembles that of a drunk
man trying to act normally.[58] To claim from this that the play is
'really' about alcohol or drugs is obviously far too reductive, but
to conceive of Dionysus exclusively as an anthropomorphised
god may not be the full picture either. To insist dogmatically on
one conception of Dionysus is in effect to follow Pentheus, and
a more authentically Dionysiac reading of the play – through
several incarnations which are not mutually exclusive even if
incompatible under the terms of pure logic – may be more
rewarding. On this reading, Dionysus is a god but also symbolises that which takes us from the everyday to altered states.
Some have gone even further and suggested that Dionysus
represents a flexibility – intellectual and otherwise – which

seeks a balance between the rational and the non-rational.[59] But given the intense individuality of Euripides' Dionysus, a purely symbolic approach, though not without validity, would be as inadequate as Pentheus' perception of the god. On any of these readings, however, it is apparent that Dionysus, whatever he is, cannot be erased from human existence.

Dionysus Dismembered: Critical Trends and the *Bacchae*

'Every reader gets the *Bacchae* he deserves'
H. Versnel, *Ter Unus,* p. 96

The *Bacchae* has always been considered one of Euripides' finest plays and has never suffered from the kinds of criticisms which bedevilled him until relatively recently. Given his stylistic and thematic tendencies (p. 10 above), he could not easily be characterised by the 'noble simplicity and serene greatness' which the nineteenth-century German critics, whose work marks the beginning of modern classical scholarship, considered the essence of Greek literature, while under the evolutionary schematisation of F. and A.W. Schlegel, whose view ultimately reflects that of Aristotle, Euripides was the wanton destroyer of an art form pioneered by Aeschylus and perfected by Sophocles.[1]

But even when appreciation of Euripides was generally in short supply, the *Bacchae*, along with the *Hippolytus*, was always admired for its apparent unity and completeness, and a subtlety of language and imagery more frequently found in Sophocles. Since a close analysis of the play yields as difficult a portrayal of Dionysus and his cult as anything in Euripides, there is an enjoyable irony in the way that the very real, 'Euripidean' difficulties of the play have been masked by its 'Sophoclean' brilliance of structure and language.[2]

Yet, rather like an irrepressible Dionysiac impulse which periodically bursts forth, the complexities of the *Bacchae* find an outlet through the remarkable number of conflicting critical approaches which the play has generated and continues to generate over the last century. At different times we have had a play whose main theme is Greek religious practice, or politics, or human psychology or drama itself; Pentheus as a puritanical tyrant or an enlightened defender of civic values; a Dionysus who is fiend, fraud or saviour.[3] To some degree, the filters through which the play has been read reflect the general tendencies of the era. The late nineteenth and earlier twentieth centuries concentrated on apparent reflections of cult in the play, while in the 1960s and 70s, criticism tended instead to focus on aspects of human psychology, sexuality and Dionysus' relationship with the feminine. Like Dionysus himself, interests of earlier eras can reappear in different disguises, and some recent criticism reconsiders Dionysus-cult as an important element of the play. Interpretations of the *Bacchae* are also influenced by assessments of Euripides' work as a whole: Arthur Verrall's 'rationalist' Euripides – a foe of religion – is the author of a very different play from that of E.R. Dodds' 'irrationalist', who does not consider reason sufficient for human virtue or happiness,[4] and the anti-rational Euripides has been especially attractive to recent generations.

Friedrich Nietzsche famously conceptualised the opposing forces of the Dionysiac and the Apollonian in *The Birth of Tragedy*.[5] Although the book barely refers to the *Bacchae*, his impression of the Dionysiac can hardly be divorced from Euripides' evocation of the god, as some representative quotation shows. ['When] the principle of reason in any of its forms appears to break down [and] we add to this horror the blissful rapture which rises up from the innermost depths of man, even of nature, as a result of the very same collapse of the *principium individuationis*,[6] we steal a glimpse into the essence of the *Dionysian*, with which we will become best acquainted through the analogy of *intoxication* ... In song and dance man expresses himself as a member of a higher communal nature ... Just as now the animals speak and the earth gives forth milk and honey ... he feels himself as god, now he himself strides forth as enraptured and uplifted as he saw the gods stride forth in dreams ... the chisel-blows of the Dionysian artist of worlds are accompanied by the sound of the Eleusinian Mysteries calling: "Do you fall to your knees, multitudes? World, do you sense the creator?"'[7]

Nietzsche bases his claims for the centrality of Dionysus to tragedy on the ancient tradition that the god's sufferings were the original subject of the genre, and argues that when this original Dionysiac power lost its dominance on stage in the later fifth century, tragedy met its end: for Nietzsche, the culprits were Euripides and his fellow intellectual Socrates, who brought 'the spectator onto the stage,' so that the divine heights of Dionysiac intensity could no longer be reached. Nietzsche's assertion recalls Aristophanes *Frogs* 952-4 in which Aristophanes' comic incarnation of Euripides claims that he has made tragedy more democratic by giving women and slaves a voice in a genre traditionally belonging to kings and heroes. Based as it apparently is on contemporary evidence, Nietzsche's claim might seem highly plausible were it not for the existence of the *Bacchae* itself, a very late fifth-century play which invokes a tremendous Dionysian power. Nietzsche attempts to minimise this discrepancy by interpreting the *Bacchae* as Euripides' belated recognition that his opposition to Dionysus had been wrong. He argues that the attitudes of old Cadmus and Tiresias to the god reflect the older and wiser playwright's final judgment but that the change of heart was too late: Euripides' earlier efforts had been too successful and tragedy, the *Bacchae* notwithstanding was, in Nietzsche's definition, dead.[8]

Many of Nietzsche's arguments are demonstrably untrue or misleading,[9] and his *a priori* decision that Euripides murdered tragedy seems to obstruct any direct appraisal of the *Bacchae* which could actually have supported parts of his thesis. The great German scholar Wilamowitz was extremely hostile to the book, but it influenced important scholars of Greek religion such as Erwin Rohde[10] and is still worth reading today, not least for the breathless grandeur of its style, even in translation. Nietzsche was one of the first modern scholars to challenge his contemporaries' view of the Greeks as rational optimists, and his radical insight that Dionysus is as much a 'cluster of psychological and social abstractions' within us as a divine force is

almost taken for granted by many scholars today.[11] The conception of Dionysus as a god who presides over, or even
symbolically represents, mental or civic disorder, sex-role or
status reversal during periods of ritual licence and the break-
down of natural, social or conceptual boundaries, not only
underlies the work of some of the most influential critics of the
Bacchae, such as Dodds, Segal and Vernant,[12] but permeates
popular culture, in which 'Dionysus' denotes a kind of archetypal rock star or religious leader, usually with indiscriminate
appetites for all manner of sexual and pharmaceutical transgressions.[13] Although recent scholars have characterised the
sensational Nietzschean Dionysus as a product of mythological
narrative and have preferred the less glamorous Dionysus of
archaeological record, as I have argued above (pp. 29-31),
disruption and paradox are not absent from Athenian
Dionysus-cult, even if bloody infanticide is not a part of it.

In the past, the atheist of popular tradition seemed to many
an unlikely author of a play which acknowledges the tremendous power of a god, and Nietzsche was not alone in viewing the
Bacchae as some kind of recantation. The theory that the play
represented Euripides' conversion to religious belief was particularly popular among Christian critics and not only held sway
far into the nineteenth century,[14] but in a much weakened form
continued to have some currency especially in French criticism,
most commonly in romantic ideas that the choruses of the
Bacchae originate from the sojourn of the 'Greek Voltaire' in
Macedonia and his longing in old age for the peace of nature
and eternal happiness gained by initiation into Dionysiac
mysteries.[15] The theory of the old atheist's final repentance
was, however, vigorously contested by Arthur Verrall in the late
nineteenth century, and, after him, by Gilbert Norwood.[16]
Verrall saw the play as a final blast against divinities who were
neither real nor worthy of belief and attempted to unmask all
the apparent miracles that the god works in it. He ascribes
Pentheus' 'mad scene' merely to drunkenness and believes that
the Dionysus whom we see for most of the play is no god but
rather a charismatic human priest who works through the
credulity of all who meet him. Pentheus' crime is his willing-

ness to punish the priest on a mere presumption of his guilt.[17] In early work, Norwood went even further in his attempts to discredit Dionysus: the liquids which spring up at the touch of the thyrsus (704-11) were, in his explanation, the products of bottles hidden in the soil![18]

The theories of Verrall and Norwood have long been out of date, but they concern a question which has been central to discussions of the *Bacchae* for well over a century. Even though few, if any, critics of the last 30 years or so would hold the nineteenth-century opinion that Euripides was more of a propagandist than a dramatist, his portrayal of Dionysus and what he does in the *Bacchae* makes it hard to banish a suspicion that Euripides intended to convey to his audience a definite opinion about the desirability of Dionysus and the religion he brings to Thebes.[19] Critics have generally focussed on Dionysus and a different Dionysus obviously yields a different Pentheus: if the play is interpreted as anything like Euripides' conversion, then Pentheus must be roundly condemned, while a view of Dionysus closer to that of Norwood will make Pentheus' hostility more reasonable. Attitudes to Tiresias are similarly polarised because he supports Dionysus. Moreover, the echoes in his speech of the language and ideas of some of the intellectuals of Euripides' day are also sometimes held to discredit his support of Dionysus and to characterise him as a sinister and untrustworthy figure, or at best a worldly cleric, who supports the new religious movement insofar as it will bolster his own power and prestige.[20] By contrast, Desmond Conacher's view of Dionysus is more favourable and his Tiresias is a respectable religious figure who is attempting to incorporate an ecstatic element into traditional religious wisdom; and given Tiresias' normal infallibility in Greek tragedy, it would be a striking break with dramatic convention to assume that his defence of Dionysus is entirely spurious.[21]

Critics' opinions may roughly be divided into four categories: either Pentheus is an admirable character fighting bravely against an evil opponent; or Pentheus is flawed but his position not unreasonable, especially given the viciousness of Dionysus' punishment; or Dionysus' actions are shocking but he is right to punish Pentheus; or, lastly, the manifold benefits of Dionysus-cult simply trump what he does to Pentheus. Norwood is the most extreme example of the first category in arguing that Pentheus is the finest character in the play, 'warm-hearted, generous, hasty in defence of his friends and of his opinions alike', whose only crime is to believe too hastily in the rumours surrounding Dionysus who is, however, not to be trusted and certainly no god. Norwood is virtually unique in this opinion of Pentheus,[22] and others who defend him do so with a more critical eye. Either Pentheus' ignorance or his role as king of Thebes are typically cited as mitigating factors. Some argue that he merely repeats what he has been told about the cult, or that he cannot know that the stranger is a god; others, that he sincerely believes Dionysus to be a dangerous force, whose acceptance will create social disruption in Thebes and that it is his duty to expel him. Pentheus' own tyrannical characteristics, or the wilfulness of his refusal to consider a different view of Dionysus are not necessarily ignored in such assessments, but the sincerity of his attempts to defend Thebes is given greater weight by these critics.[23] Some critics rationalise Pentheus' attitude to the god by comparing it with the Romans' ban on Dionysiac cult in 186 BCE (Livy 39.9-18), or with Athenian ambivalence, if not active hostility, to the foreign cults that flooded into Athens during the Peloponnesian War.[24] In general, however, it is less easy to find Pentheus sympathetic than to condemn Dionysus' cruelty, and it may be that the peculiar horror of his death makes critics retrospectively consider him a more sympathetic character than he would otherwise have been.[25]

By contrast, many critics consider Dionysus' revenge justified by Pentheus' behaviour. Although the late Victorian scholar Sandys interpreted Pentheus' interest in Dionysus' effects on the sexual mores of the Theban women as proper concern for his city's womenfolk, and a recent reading interprets it in the context of his kingly duty to the Theban males whose conjugal rights Dionysus has violated,[26] in the criticism of the last few decades, his actions tend to be interpreted at best as prurience and at worst as signs of his own psychological peculiarity, both of which make his position indefensible. Moreover, his behaviour is frequently that of the stereotypical tyrant who is always an object of condemnation in Athenian tragedy.[27] Thus, with varying degrees of emphasis, many critics more sympathetic to Dionysus consider Pentheus' apparent psychological peculiarities and tyrannical tendencies 'sins' for which he is duly punished, while another, less prominent, strain of criticism regards his fate as punishment for religious failings.[28]

Although it is not a contradiction to believe both that the play portrays a transgressor who is punished and also that the punishment is excessive, other critics (in differing degrees) claim that the god offers Pentheus many opportunities for repentance before the final blow: since he rejects them, his punishment is just.[29] Conacher and Burnett contrast Aphrodite's obsessional desire for revenge in the *Hippolytus* with Dionysus' merely conditional revenge which offers Pentheus chances for redemption until relatively late in the play.[30] Conacher even claims that Dionysus' actions are proper because Dionysiac religion illustrates a basic truth that human life needs to contain not just reason but a state of passive receptivity or 'rest' which is Dionysus' domain. Since this 'rest' is essential for human well-being, we must willingly embrace it: if we do not, we will be forced to do so and Pentheus' punishment represents this truth.[31]

Conacher leads us to one argument frequently used in favour of Dionysus: when his religion is not persecuted, it brings its adherents huge benefits – emotional release, peace, and unity with fellow worshippers and with the natural world. Yet Winnington Ingram – perhaps influenced by what he saw of the mass rallies in favour of Hitler and Mussolini in Germany and Italy while he was writing *Euripides and Dionysus* – saw the emotional release brought about by the loss of an individual self in a larger group as dangerous. Certainly, Dionysus benefits his worshippers, but they also lose their sense of reality and their intellect and individualism, as they succumb to a crowd mentality, a cult of emotion which tends to dehumanise. Since Dionysus' worshippers live intensely in the present moment, they ignore the considerations of past and future which, for Winnington Ingram, distinguish a civilised human life from a merely animal existence. For Winnington Ingram, Dionysus' insistence on worship from everyone makes him not a democrat but merely a leveller and enemy of the noble effort that leads to higher status.[32]

Since the *Bacchae* portrays the cult of Dionysus both as a religious fanaticism which destroys reason and as a manifestation of a truly divine power, it is impossible with any sense of certainty to rule out one set of interpretations in favour of another, except in their extreme manifestations.[33] Such ambiguity may be innate to a god whose patronage extends to wine and drama. Theatre is real action taking place before its audience, yet it is not literally real since it brings before them a story whose outcome is already pre-determined. When drunk, what I perceive is real in that I perceive it at the time, but it may not be what I perceive when sober. Both wine and drama create illusion, a fresh vision of reality which can be enlightenment or delusion, and Dionysus works between illusion and reality. He is both a culture hero and a threat to civilisation, who brings liberation and/or chaos: the only sure thing is that he cannot be ignored.[34] Since he embodies contradictions of joy and horror, insight and madness, he cannot fail to be ambiguous when viewed through narrower human conceptions of right and wrong.[35] Of all the general views of Dionysus offered, this is the one which seems most attractive in its 'Dionysiac' quality of incorporating a multitude of apparent contradictions in the portrayal of Dionysus and Pentheus. Yet even this one fails to convince on every level, because the truth about what Dionysus can do is troubling. It is a terrible god whose greatness is manifested in destruction and misery, and ultimately it must be acknowledged that the *Bacchae* never entirely resolves the distinction between the two images of divinity – one, a mysterious object of cult, the other, a personal, vengeful force – which live in uneasy tension with one another.[36]

Dionysus and the symbolic

From here we return to questions raised at the end of Chapter 4, which in fact recur in every Greek tragedy in which a god takes a dominant role. Is this play literally about an offended divine being who punishes a human for not having worshipped him enough? Is it, as Conacher and others imply, about the dangers of repressing fundamental human instincts? Or is it somewhere between these two poles of interpretation? Because of Euripides' long-standing reputation as an intellectual who questioned the existence of the traditional gods, it has seemed incredible to some that he could have endorsed the literal existence and power of a god who works miracles or destruction. The instinct of many critics, therefore, has been to look behind the traditional divine framework and to consider Dionysus less as a personified god than as a symbolic representation, whether externalising Pentheus' own repressed longings or some more abstract concept, such as the overwhelming power of human instinctual urges. Others, uneasy about what seems like a demotion of an incarnate god, accept that Pentheus is destroyed, not by something within him which the figure of the god symbolises, but by Dionysus' influence acting on him externally.[37] Some earlier critics even try to have it both ways by suggesting that Euripides wrote for two audiences: the clods whose belief was literal and the intellectuals of his own type who would understand what 'Dionysus' really was.[38]

The question goes straight to the heart of Greek religion itself, because there is some truth in the idea that the Greek gods represent certain conditions, forces or other aspects of human existence – love, wine, the sea and so on – and that their very nature as gods *of* wine, or the sea, or love gives them a symbolic dimension. Winnington Ingram, whose Greek gods essentially personify elements in the natural world, argues that such deification endows with human qualities things which are not bound by human moral sense and in order to explain the suffering these deified elements inevitably bring, the Greeks had to create reasons for the gods' just anger.[39] It is certainly true that many genres of Greek literature, especially tragedy, are deeply marked by a process of justification and explanation for suffering and Sourvinou-Inwood has recently argued that tragedy originated as an exploration through religion of the conditions under which humans must live. Although suffering is inevitable, some explanation, however imperfect, of its causes at least provides reassurance that the world is not randomly evil and since Greek religion has no devil, everything, however bad, must come from the gods.[40] In tragedy, suffering is never random bad luck nor is human motivation usually sufficient as a cause of tragic suffering. Rather, the character of the sufferer is fatally involved in circumstances over which he has no control: disaster is justified or explained through an appeal to a force which is, or has turned, unfriendly, and that force is represented anthropomorphically as a divinity.

The relationship between the characters of Dionysus and Pentheus in the scenes in which Pentheus is overwhelmed and destroyed by the god undoubtedly lends itself to symbolic readings of various kinds[41] and one obvious reason for modern interest in such readings is that Dionysus-cult is no longer a part of living religious culture.[42] Euripides' audience, however, were watching the play in the Theatre of Dionysus and had participated in the Dionysus-rituals preceding the dramatic performances. Moreover, from a literary perspective, Euripides' Dionysus closely resembles the anthropomorphic divinities of Homer: modern critics of Homer are less uncomfortable than many critics of Euripides with the idea that the audience of such an ancient and traditional genre accepted the interventions of the gods as literal events rather than symbolic manifestations of something else. Such considerations make it less likely that an ancient audience would have considered Dionysus *primarily* as an externalised symbol of a natural force or of internal human psychological motivation. Indeed, a symbol of nature or psychological instincts should be neutral, rather than actively vengeful, but Dionysus' vengeance is personally directed against Pentheus and those who deny his divinity:[43] his acts are those of an individual being, not some neutral symbol, nor could a purely symbolic god produce the factual miracles on which the characters of the play frequently comment (the Verrall– Norwood idea of mass hypnosis notwithstanding).

Even so, some recent critics argue that the totality of Dionysus is beyond human knowledge and, if so, we *can* only experience him indirectly and symbolically.[44] Completely to reject Dionysus' symbolic dimension necessitates the abandonment of much fascinating critical work on the play even if his symbolic element cannot fully explain or contain him. The influence of this Nietzschean, symbolic god was strong, for example, on Walter Otto, the scholar whose theory of Dionysus as the god of epiphanies and polarities is fundamental to many interpretations of the *Bacchae*.[45] French scholars have also frequently conceptualised Dionysus as representative of opposites and 'otherness', so that in Jean-Paul Vernant's formulation, to the male, Dionysus will be female, to the Greek, he will be barbarian, to humans, divine and thus always Other, forever changing into whatever one least knows.[46] This portrayal of Dionysus could reasonably be called standard critical opinion at the time of writing, but it is not the only currently influential interpretation. Richard Seaford has vigorously disputed the validity of the Nietzschean interpretation in favour of an interpretation which centres on Dionysus as the object of mystery cult and champion of democratic rule at Thebes, and this important challenge to orthodoxy will be discussed in greater detail below.[47]

Although majority opinion today would accept that Dionysus, whatever he represents or is, cannot be neatly pigeonholed, it is a striking feature of criticism of the play that, perhaps more than any other Euripidean drama, it has been the recipient of interpretative methodologies which act as a kind of prism through which it is viewed. Although I will treat each one separately for clarity's sake, they are not entirely separable from one another: a speech or action which is psychologically significant through one filter will be just as religiously significant through another.[48]

Ritual, structuralism and anthropology

In the early twentieth century, ritual was a very popular framework for understanding the play. Gilbert Murray and the 'Cambridge Ritualist' school argued that its structure reflected the rituals of the Year-Spirit who was associated with Dionysus. In this formulation, the Year-Spirit (represented by Dionysus) comes to prominence and is killed by an enemy (represented by Pentheus) who, being a murderer, must in turn be killed by an avenger who is in fact the resurrected Year-Spirit.[49] Although the theory of the Year-Spirit is now discredited,[50] the ritualists' interest in anthropology as an interpretative filter for the play strongly influenced E.R. Dodds' classic commentary and in some ways foreshadowed the structuralist methodology which has dominated scholarship on Greek tragedy and society for the past 25 years. It is a basic tenet of structuralist criticism of tragedy that tragedy dramatises myths in order to explore fundamental structures and institutions – especially sacrifice, marriage and agriculture – in Greek society, and to examine the analogies between them, with a view to showing how their proper performance can guarantee a healthy community and investigating what happens when they break down, as they do in tragedy.[51] Greek myth is 'good to think with' both because its characters are like us and unlike us, offering the closeness needed for empathy and the distance needed for reflection, and also because a series of polarities between male and female, foreign and citizen, self and other, god and human and so on runs through the myths. Athenian tragedy explores the shifting relationships between these polarities and often uses the forms and language of institutions fundamental to society as a framework for such explorations. When these institutions are violated or inverted in tragedy, the emotional shock of the violation rouses the audience to ask questions about their institutions and the assumptions behind them.[52]

Dionysus' quintessential nature as a threat to the hierarchical system of polarities on which Pentheus' rigid order rests makes the play apparently tailor-made for a structuralist perspective.[53] Linguistic reversals are central to it: verbs of seeing, hunting and suffering move from active to passive voices as Pentheus the spy and hunter becomes the spied-upon and hunted. Since Euripides' audience can hardly have been unaware of these reversals, it is possible that, unlike interpretations which rely on psychological or symbolic readings of the text, both of which are so grounded in our own cultural context that their validity as tools for exploring an ancient play must be uncertain, structuralist criticism might offer insights into an ancient audience's understanding of the important points of the play. Many critics have uncovered patterns of opposition and reversal in the play which go much deeper than basic divisions of gender or nationality, and have discussed the multiple ways in which institutions of fundamental importance to the Greek city are turned upside down (603, 741, 753) by Dionysus. Under his auspices, the mother traditionally in charge of laying out the dead body of her child is instead a perpetrator of the murder itself, while Cadmus gives a funeral speech fit for a warrior-king even though Pentheus failed to become such a king.[54] For Seaford, a division between the genders is basic to the structure of the city-state: although he is generally sceptical of the Nietzschean Dionysus, his Dionysus still has some elements in common with the earlier conception of the god as a figure who unites logically contradictory characteristics by both threatening this gender division and healing it at its end when his divinity is finally acknowledged.[55]

The institution of sacrifice is particularly prone to inversion and violation in tragedy because it is so central to Greek society. Sacrifice defines the place of beasts, men and gods in the Greek hierarchy: beasts eat raw flesh, men eat the beasts' cooked flesh of the sacrifice and the gods enjoy the smoke from the cooked meat.[56] Thus the sacrifice that goes wrong, so that a human being is briefly made into a beast as the world's order turns frighteningly fluid – is especially powerful for an ancient audience. The theme of perverted sacrifice has been interpreted variously by critics. Helene Foley compares the structure of Pentheus' march to death with the structure of a sacrifice, and views its significance in dramatic terms, as a way of emphasising the horror of what happens to him. By contrast, another strain of interpretation takes the perverted sacrifice as a historical reflection or distortion of actual Greek religious practices, using Pentheus' progress in the second half of the *Bacchae* as evidence for original sacrificial rituals from which tragedy was born: this kind of interpretation has elements in common with the Ritualists' theory of the *Bacchae* as a version of the Year-Spirit story.[57]

5. Dionysus Dismembered: Critical Trends and the Bacchae

Walter Burkert has argued that religion originates from the aggressive instincts of primitive human beings and that killing is central to religion. In its simplest summary, aggression between individuals in the group is instead diverted onto an animal in the hunt: the anxieties arising from the violent death of the animal eventually give rise to religious ritual. The ritual death of an animal in the sacrifice clearly parallels its death in the hunt. Myth is related to ritual and 'names what the ritual intends', [58] so that whereas hunting and sacrifice direct violence safely onto an animal, the myth can speak directly of a human victim. Burkert posits an intimate connection between violence, hunting and sacrifice, all of which are prominent elements in Euripides' treatment of Pentheus in the *Bacchae*. René Girard goes even further.[59] He suggests that all festivities commemorate an original 'sacrificial crisis', a collective act of group violence against an individual, which is later reinterpreted by the people to reclaim the original act of violence as an act against a more suitable victim (a sacrificed animal). The loss of control leading to the original act of violence becomes instead festivity, a more benevolent suspension of the normal hierarchies of life. Moreover, the responsibility for loss of human control is comfortingly transferred to an angry god. Girard takes Athenian tragedy itself as evidence for his theory and the *Bacchae* in particular as a play about the sacrificial crisis and the violent beginnings of the Dionysiac ritual, as it traces the 'festival that goes wrong' (127), from a harmonious elimination of differences to a violent non-differentiation, where even the distinctions between beast, man and god are horribly blurred. For Girard, Pentheus' murder ultimately resolves the crisis at Thebes which the god has provoked by being insufficiently honoured. Once he is killed, peace and harmony will return to the city as the god is worshipped there once more.

A major attraction of Burkert's and Girard's theories is that they incorporate so many motifs of the *Bacchae* – hunting, human sacrifice and a sudden reversal from joy to hideous violence directed against one individual who is the target of a mass group action. In the light of the ancient tradition that Dionysus was the original subject of tragedy, there is an especial attraction in imagining that the play somehow reflects (distorted) religious history. Few of us have ever experienced mob violence such as Euripides describes and it is portrayed so vividly in the *Bacchae* that it is tempting to imagine a distant and primitive past when such things did occur, especially since it is fairly certain that details such as the clothing of Pentheus, his perch on the tree and pelting with stones and branches genuinely do reflect Greek ritual practices.[60]

Unfortunately, the reasoning of Girard in particular is circular: having set up his theory of the sacrificial crisis as the background to the *Bacchae*, he claims later that the play offers evidence to support the theory,[61] and on occasion treats it almost as though it were an anthropological documentary rather than a work of imaginative fiction. Since the relationship between the myths of Dionysus and the practices of Dionysiac ritual is so complex, a theory which uses the *Bacchae* to explain ancient religious history must be treated cautiously.[62] After all, if an adaptation of the *Bacchae* used language associated with the breaking of the bread in a Roman Catholic Mass to describe the rending of Pentheus, the play would neither be a Mass, nor recreate the first Mass: instead, the familiar cultural and religious institution of the Mass would be a framework for exploring Pentheus' shocking death.

A somewhat more convincing attempt to see a reflection of Dionysiac ritual in the play, and important because it challenges the Nietzschean view which has dominated interpretation of the *Bacchae*, is the work of Richard Seaford, who argues that the play cannot be properly understood without an understanding that it contains multiple references to rituals of an Athenian Dionysiac mystery cult.[63] Whereas the Nietzschean Dionysus is conceptualised as the god who disrupts normality by combining opposites such as male and female, the life force and death and so on, Seaford suggests that the god's apparently contradictory characteristics reflect typical elements of initiation rituals. For example, the initiate is commonly imagined as 'dying' (letting go of his or her previously uninitiated life) and being 'reborn' as a member of the cult, thereby combining death and life during the period of initiation. Similarly,

Dionysus' combination of male and female could reflect the temporary transvestism which is a frequent feature of initiation rites.[64] Seaford argues that there are simply too many references to initiatory practices in the action and language of the *Bacchae* for the links to be coincidental and that initiation ritual must be central to a proper interpretation of the play. He concludes that the play tells the story of the foundation of the Dionysiac mysteries at Thebes and enacts the myth which in its turn has been shaped by the practices of those mysteries.[65] Seaford links the religious elements of the play with a political dimension by arguing that Dionysus' triumph is the triumph of a new democracy as Dionysus the democrat-god destroys the Theban royal family and establishes a new political order at Thebes (cf. p. 97 below).

Seaford's work is not universally accepted, partly because the evidence for a developed Dionysiac mystery cult at Athens at the time of the writing of the play is not absolutely clear, but also because, although Seaford acknowledges in theory the validity of other methods of interpretation, his *Commentary* focusses intently on cult as a kind of master-key to the interpretation of the play.[66] If the play essentially dramatises the facts of Dionysus-cult, it is hard to see how any other reading, especially along more symbolically- or psychologically-oriented lines can coexist very easily with this interpretation: the *Bacchae* is such a complex play, however, that recent critics tend to resist the idea that one specific theory is capable of ironing out all its complexities. For this reason I would prefer to interpret the undoubted existence of elements of ritual in the *Bacchae* as more generally a religious background against which their perversion in the climax of the play appears all the more disturbing.

Some critics have seen a further religious significance in Pentheus' fate and describe him as a scapegoat. It is true that the circumstances of his death share features with rituals familiar elsewhere, in which some surrogate dies (often by stoning) on behalf of the city, but the scapegoat has a very specific religious significance as the individual creature on whom all the woes of the city are placed so that it can be renewed.[67] Although Seaford and others argue that Pentheus' death functions in a similar way to restore Thebes, the devastation which Dionysus brings on Thebes seems to make this an excessively optimistic interpretation of the end of the *Bacchae*.[68]

Henk Versnel[69] considers the *Bacchae* in the context of contemporary Athenian religion and shows that a play concerning the introduction of a new god was of more than theoretical or symbolic interest in the late fifth century, as Athens faced the challenge of assimilation of a number of foreign cults – including that of Sabazius, an Eastern god whose worship resembled that of Dionysus – into the city. That these new cults found adherents, as well as enemies, in Athens illustrates an inherent tension in religion – reflected in the *Bacchae* – between safe, institutionalised religious forms necessary for the stability of the city, and a potentially disruptive desire for intensity and excitement. Versnel argues that Pentheus' hostility to Dionysus would have struck a familiar chord with many of the audience who faced the dangers of incorporating foreign gods into their city, and the case of Socrates shows that some who introduced new cults could indeed be tried for impiety. Yet, unlike those for whom Pentheus is justified by such considerations, Versnel argues that since Dionysus is obviously not a new god at Athens, Pentheus must be wrong to reject him.

Politics

Religious ritual, though one of the oldest and most productive sources of interpretation of the play, is not the only filter through which it has been seen. Political interpretations of the *Bacchae* have run the gamut from very broadly political readings which situate it in a general conflict between the claims of the group and those of the individual[70] to specific attempts to tie it to fifth-century Athenian politics. Some earlier critics, particularly in France, interpreted the play as a political allegory, setting Pentheus the representative of the city against a Dionysus who embodies excessive political ambition, or who even represents Alcibiades, a politician whose name was a byword for unscrupulous ambition.[71] Such explicit analogies are out of fashion, but Seaford once again challenges orthodoxy in arguing that the *Bacchae* traces the collapse of an unsuccessful royal family and endorses at its end the democratically-ruled city-state under its patron Dionysus, the democratic god who hates all distinctions of status.[72] Seaford again disputes the validity of the Nietzschean Dionysus of unresolvable contradiction by denying that he is a paradoxical figure in his combination of benevolence (to humanity) and cruelty (to Pentheus). For Seaford, he would only be this contradictory figure if Pentheus truly represented the order of the city which Dionysus then destroys. If, however, Pentheus is merely a tyrant, then Dionysus' triumph is the triumph of the democratically-ruled state and his dominance is commendable. Seaford also argues that the story expresses a troublesome tension between men and women, as the male Pentheus resists the god whose followers are female: again, the triumph of the god enables the resolution of the tension. Seaford's view of Dionysus, politically no less than religiously, is optimistic:[73] not only does it gloss over the fact that Pentheus was actually tricked into his death by the god but it also suggests that Pentheus and his family are not worthy of pity, in spite of Euripides' evident attempts to evoke such feelings (1118-21, 1352ff.).

Psychological and symbolic approaches

At this point we move from religious and political interpretations to those which depend more on Euripides' language and imagery. Aristotle claimed that action, rather than any psychological characteristics of its characters, was primary in tragedy because one could have an action without personified characters but not vice versa (*Poetics* 1450a16 ff.). His claim is based on far more evidence than we will ever have, and must always be remembered when discussing individual character in Greek tragedy, but even he goes on to admit that characters must be individualised sufficiently for their actions to be plausible in the context of the plot. A debate has traditionally taken place in the context of these two statements between those who believe that Greek tragedy contains examples of recognisable individuals and those who consider that it is futile and anachronistic to interpret Greek tragedy as though it were Shakespearian drama. The debate has expanded in a series of arguments and counter-arguments from critics for whom Euripides' characters rather resembled those of a modern novel,[74] to German scholars such as Howald and Zürcher,[75] who claimed that Euripides was more concerned to achieve particular effects in individual episodes than to create consistent characters. Critics, especially in Britain, have typically been wary of imposing on Greek tragedy concepts of individual psychology,[76] but recent opinion is more open to the idea that Euripides, more than the other tragedians, was interested in creating individuals. In Collard's formulation, Euripides, unlike Sophocles or Aeschylus, gives his characters self-examination and self-deception, and projects personality in ways that anticipate modern psychoanalysis.[77] Long before such ideas were generally viewed as respectable in Euripidean criticism, however, they were applied implicitly to the *Bacchae*, so that not only was Euripides' portrayal of Pentheus assumed to be consistent but certain psychological descriptions were applied to him which would have been far more controversial if applied to other tragic characters.

A distinction may be made between criticism which specifically considers Pentheus as an individual case study and that which originates from the Nietzschean view that the play externalises more general psychological motivations. Although in practice it is hard to make a complete distinction between these because the exact nature of what Dionysus symbolises is disputed, the latter more than the former critical approach has won greater acceptance among critics, given the obvious circularity of applying terminology to Greek drama based on the theories of Freud, whose theories were influenced by Greek drama.[78] Psychological 'diagnosis' of Pentheus has, however, a surprisingly long pedigree, going back as far as 1844, when J.A. Hartung dubbed him a voyeur, while even such great figures in the canon of classical scholarship as Wilamowitz characterise Pentheus as a 'dark puritan whose passion is compounded of horror and unconscious desire.'[79] Certain modern critics have diagnosed Pentheus as sexually repressed, afraid of castration, or a transvestite,[80] and though it is methodologically dubious to equate the experience of modern cross-dressers with a change of clothing imposed on Pentheus by a god, the fact that such a comparison can be made, in extended form, is a mark of Euripides' remarkable insight. It is doubtful that Sophoclean or Aeschylean characters could bear the weight of such an analysis. Indeed, a persuasive article by the classically and psychoanalytically-trained George Devereux offers multiple correspondences between Cadmus' 'cure' of Agave's madness and modern therapeutic techniques.[81] On the other hand, apparently recognisable phenomena may be misleading when they are taken from a culture so different from ours. Pentheus might look like a voyeur, but, as Justina Gregory notes, whereas for moderns the voyeur's state of mind is primary, the ancients emphasised result over intention. Many myths focus on an involuntary sight of the forbidden because the fact of seeing is more important than the reasons for seeing, and so, for Gregory, Pentheus' mistake has nothing to do with voyeurism but originates in an excessive valuation of the secular over the religious which makes him unable to recognise the stranger's powers for what they really are.[82]

Any psychological dimension of the play must always remain slightly beyond a firm critical grasp, because it depends so heavily on the symbolic nature of Euripides' language and imagery.[83] Since symbolism is in the eye of the beholder, a great degree of variation among critics exists, both on which events represent inner processes and also on exactly what those inner processes are. Some scholars argue that the *Bacchae* is partly a play about drama itself (pp. 100-2 below), and Segal has discussed at length the relationship between dramatic performance and the spectators' unconscious, in the 'dream world' of the stage, where fears and fantasies can be worked out by means of rhetorical transformations and symbolic displacements effected by language, as we view what we do not normally let ourselves see or hear.[84] One might almost dub disentangling the symbolism of the *Bacchae* as itself Dionysiac: what one accepts as symbolic, and what it symbolises, reflects one's own general position as a critic (and arguably, one's own psychological make-up as well: cf. *Bacchae* 314-18.) For example, even the most sceptical critics accept that Agave's murder of Pentheus is prefigured symbolically in the rending of the herds, but not everyone will accept that Pentheus' rending represents in material form his psychological collapse, or that his wrestling with the bull (a standard emblem of virility and sexuality) symbolises his struggles with his own desires.[85] What, then, of Segal's suggestion that the landscape Pentheus enters can be seen as a symbolic projection of the female body and especially the mysterious body of the mother? Our language plays a part in shaping such readings: Segal's 'intrusion into a moist grassy hollow' to describe Pentheus' arrival at the glen at 1051-2 makes sexual symbolism highly prominent, but a differently-worded description would not necessarily bring such symbolism to the fore.[86] More convincing, perhaps, is the suggestion that Pentheus' fate symbolises a failed passage to maturity as Segal – perhaps Euripides' most Dionysiac critic in the abundance of his interpretations – has also argued. The Greeks were fascinated by the figure of the young man, or ephebe, on the edge of mature adulthood and the potential dangers of his transition from boyhood to full maturity. Such figures appear frequently in Greek literature and Segal suggests that the images of being hunted, devoured, caught and trapped by a powerful maternal figure which appear in the *Bacchae* symbolically represent the dangers attendant on the ephebe's passage to full maturity and the anxieties of the community over this crucial period in the lives of its young men.[87] It is, of course, entirely possible to discuss the play coherently and convincingly without any appeal to psychological or symbolic interpretations,[88] but to deny such approaches entirely excludes consideration of some fascinating scholarship, even if its conclusions sometimes have more to say to moderns than to Euripides' ancient audience.

Metatheatre

The theatre-god breaks down barriers between reality and illusion since theatre itself confuses the two by creating illusion to convey truth. Critics of recent years have suggested that

5. Dionysus Dismembered: Critical Trends and the Bacchae

Euripides is deliberately drawing attention to theatrical illusions in his own play and, in particular, Helene Foley has argued that, since access to him can only be indirect and symbolic, to honour and comprehend Dionysus demands the exploration and acceptance of theatrical concepts such as illusion, transformation and symbol. Those like Pentheus who cannot understand this fail to understand the god and will be destroyed.[89] Particularly rich in meaning in this context are the theatrical elements of Dionysus' mask and of the costumes which his worshippers wear. Several times, the play draws deliberate attention to the god's smiling mask. If, as has been suggested, a smile was typical of divine masks, then through theatrical convention Euripides conveys a truth about the stranger's divinity which the audience understands but which the wilfully ignorant Pentheus does not. All masks are ambiguous between reality and illusion and between accessibility and alienation. Dionysus' mask is more ambiguous than most in disguising a human actor playing a god who is playing a mortal, and in embodying a human power to create symbols while also revealing the god's sinister Otherness.[90] As the play unfolds, his smile remains constant in form but changes radically in meaning, from the smile of the captured 'beast' at 438-9 to the god's cruel smile of revenge at 1021. Its shifts in meaning illustrate Tiresias' claim that what you see in Dionysus is what you bring to him (314-18).[91]

Pentheus' progress to his end has also been described as a play within a play. Dionysus as 'stage manager' controls the details of his costume and action, and even rehearses him in his new role as a Maenad.[92] When Pentheus is transformed by the robing scene from king to victim, we see the power of tragic costume to reveal the truth through disguise and illusion. The Chorus too have a metatheatrical dimension in the play in the inherent self-reflexiveness of their playing worshippers of Dionysus in a Dionysiac festival. Even the genres of tragedy and comedy are blurred, so that the play ends with a tragic death which is, at least at first, joyfully celebrated by Agave in the manner of the festivities which commonly occur at the end of Attic comedy. Moreover, there is a parallel between her return to sanity and the process of recognition which takes place within each spectator as we attempt to integrate what we have seen on stage into the reality of our own experience.[93] Even the earthquake scene, in which the Chorus describe the destruction of Pentheus' palace while the technological limitations of the Greek theatre necessitate that little or nothing probably happens on stage, has been interpreted metatheatrically: the tension between what is said and what is shown may compel the audience to consider the power of dramatic illusion and the symbolic dimension of all stage events.[94] Yet, as Seaford reminds us, everything in the play which seems to have theatrical or psychological resonance can also be interpreted, and tragedy itself has a deep connection with religious ritual: thus Agave's revelry resembles the end of a sacrifice as well as the end of a comedy.[95] The god dislikes distinctions (206) and there is something undeniably fitting about our inability as critics to make clear distinctions between these multiple interpretative filters through which the play has been viewed over the last century.

6

Singing! Orgies! Wine! Women! Song![1]

Both the plays of Euripides and the figure of Dionysus were highly popular in the centuries after Euripides' death. Later literature is said to contain more quotations from Euripides than anyone else except Homer and Menander, while Dionysus, as triumphant civilising force and god of relaxed refinement, who paraded through the world winning hearts and minds with his gift of wine and an army of Maenads and satyrs, was used by Alexander the Great and later aspiring rulers of the East as a divine role model.[2] Moreover, the erotic possibilities offered by the portrayal of the god with his Maenads made them popular subjects of art for centuries.[3] In the Middle Ages, as Christianity came to dominate European religious life, Dionysus' importance recedes but does not disappear, and as late as 692 CE, church fathers in Constantinople had to prohibit their flocks from dancing, wearing masks or women's clothes and invoking Dionysus at the vintage.[4] Dionysus as the incarnation of boozy jollity presides over pastoral merrymaking in Renaissance and Baroque painting and a multitude of eponymous wine-bars in contemporary culture.[5] Such portrayals essentially ignore the darker side of his power which is central to Euripides' play, and this chapter will concentrate on the god in his more complex incarnation in post-Euripidean versions and productions of the play.

Euripides' plays remained popular in the theatrical life of the fourth century, during which the politician Lycurgus passed a law establishing official texts of Aeschylus, Sophocles and Euripides to be used in dramatic revivals. These survived for nearly 2,000 years before the advent of the printing press by a lengthy and precarious process of hand-copying, during which it was easy for errors and omissions to creep in: these texts are the distant ancestors of those which we use today. Literary and inscriptional evidence shows that the *Bacchae* retained a place at Rome, in adaptations by Pacuvius (*Pentheus*, third-second century BCE) and Accius (*Bacchae*, second century BCE), while in texts of the first century BCE, Dionysiac experience symbolises uncontrolled ecstasy, whether poetic (e.g. Horace *Odes* 2.19) or menacing (Virgil *Aeneid* 4.300ff., 7.385ff.).[6] The events of the play were supposedly even imitated in real life: Plutarch (*Life of Crassus* 33) alleges that after the failure of the Roman general Crassus' campaign in 53 BCE, lines 1169-71 of the play were recited at the Parthian court by an actor dressed as Agave using Crassus' own head as prop. Nonnus, a poet of the fifth century CE, devotes books 44-6 of his *Dionysiaca*, a 20,000 line-long account of the god's adventures, to paraphrasing and amplifying Euripides. Nonnus heightens the impiety of Pentheus so that he claims that he is both the offspring and the consort of gods (44.170ff.). His final speech is also extended, as is Agave's declaration of remorse (46.192-208; 283-319) in which she asks for madness again since sanity is so dreadful, laments that she will not see Pentheus married and begs him to forgive her. In a gruesome climax, she even asks Dionysus for a cup so that she may pour him a libation of Pentheus' blood. Whether any of this replicates a speech of Agave originally in Euripides but now lost in the gaps in our text at 1300 and 1329 must remain uncertain (cf. pp. 48-9 above). But in a notable departure from the gloom of Euripides' ending, Dionysus takes active pity on them and offers Agave and her sisters wine, a potion of forgetfulness and cheering oracles for the future.

Greek literature retained some place in European culture long after the end of the ancient pre-Christian world, and even some of the early Christian fathers who inveighed against the works of the pagans were nonetheless fascinated by them. Clement of Alexandria (*c.* 200 CE) condemns Bacchic ecstasy as counterfeit, yet also believes that it prefigures the real ecstasy attainable through Christ (*Protrepticus* 12.92). The appeal to medieval Christians of a god born of a woman and a divinity connected with wine and (at least in some versions) who dies and rises again is obvious.[7] Dionysiac iconography influences early Christian iconography, and the twelfth-century *Christus Patiens* uses lines from Agave's lamentation over Pentheus' corpse to express Mary's lamentation over Jesus' body. As with Agave's lament in Nonnus, it is, however, impossible to go beyond generalities in recovering the content of the missing portions of our text from the later play. The *Bacchae* survived in manuscript copies until its first printing in the Aldine edition of the play in 1503.[8] Early Latin translations, such as that of Martirano of Cosenza (1556), helped to propagate knowledge of Greek tragedy[9] but there is little real interest in Euripides before the seventeenth century, and even then the *Bacchae* was not especially popular.

In fact, the play was considered so violent that it was performed only sporadically before the 1960s. In the United States, there were no productions on the commercial stage before then, and only a handful of college productions,[10] while some statistics from Oxford's Archive of Performances of Greek and Roman Drama tell their own tale. From 1886-1964, 40 productions or adaptations worldwide of the *Bacchae* are listed, with 17 in the United Kingdom[11] and 12 in the United States: by contrast, from 1965-2004, a staggering 199 versions are listed worldwide, some 48 in the United Kingdom along with another 47 in the United States.[12] The popularity of the *Bacchae* soared during the 1960s, as the conflict between Dionysus and Pentheus easily – if simplistically – came to symbolise that between those who rebelled against social norms and embraced sexual and chemical experimentation and those who upheld traditional modes of authority. The play has been frequently performed and adapted ever since, although different periods have stressed different elements in the text and adaptors tend to focus on one or two themes to the exclusion of many others.[13] The following pages offer a survey of some of the most interesting versions and analyse typical trends of adaptation and performance. This survey is not exhaustive, given the multitude and international breadth of performances of the *Bacchae* especially over the last three decades,[14] but it will alert readers to some of the many 'descendants' of

Euripides and offer a starting point for further exploration of traditions of performance and adaptation of this most versatile play.

The elements of the *Bacchae* which typically receive most immediate attention from modern audiences are those of chaos, irrationality, violence and sexuality, especially gender ambiguity.[15] Because of the play's apparent modernity, it has often been the recipient of experimental treatments which have little in common with the 'sheets and sandals' traditional style of ancient dramatic production. The most famous version of this type is *Dionysus in 69* by the New York-based director Richard Schechner.[16] Its text arose from improvisational workshops over a period of many months[17] and its form was different every night, both because of its fluid cast – during its run, four different actors (including one woman) played Dionysus, and each used his or her own form of the dialogue and (to some extent) of the order of events – and because of the emphasis it placed on audience participation. For Schechner, theatre was to be 'part celebration, part therapy, part ecstasy and part almost a religious sense of mystery at the heart of the self.'[18] In some ways, this is an especially appropriate view of a play dramatising a religion in which worshippers identify so closely with each other and their god, and yet a play which *portrays* Dionysiac experience is very different from one which demands direct participation. Euripides' play describes scenes of savage ugliness and chaos, but its violence is portrayed in language of unparalleled beauty and the conventions surrounding Attic tragic performance would have discouraged Euripides' audience from literally trying to participate in the action on stage. In Schechner's production, however, it was always possible that the audience would storm the stage, and the elements of convention and control in action and language were much less dominant.

Moreover, whereas the suspicions of Euripides' Pentheus about the Maenads' practices are wrong, Schechner's Dionysiac religion is explicitly sexual. The beauty of Euripides' Dionysus is overshadowed by his coercive, ugly side in this adaptation and this emphasis influences the language of the play: although

Schechner uses some 600 lines of Euripides, often roughly in sequence with the original, he dispenses with the beauty of Euripides' poetry. Schechner's version is also strongly metatheatrical and uses Euripides' text itself as a means of emphasising the power reversal between Dionysus and Pentheus. At the start of the play, the rigid Pentheus keeps closely to his Euripidean lines while Dionysus speaks freely with less reliance on a Euripidean model, but by the end, Pentheus is unable to follow his Euripidean lines, as though his personality has been destroyed, while Dionysus has grown into his full divinity and his words become closer to those of the Euripidean original. In one version of the script Dionysus responds to Cadmus' complaint that the gods should not resemble humans in anger by updating Euripides' 'Long ago, Zeus decreed these things' to 'Long ago, Euripides wrote these things', so that Euripides and Zeus are neatly assimilated as arbiters of Pentheus' fate.

Nudity, profanity, vast amounts of stage blood and an explicit portrayal of Pentheus as a repressed gay man helped to make *Dionysus in 69* notorious: after one performance the entire cast was charged with indecent exposure by Penthean local authorities.[19] Although it is now remembered for its more sensational elements, shock was not Schechner's only aim: the political background of the Vietnam war and a comparison of America and Thebes – both oppressively strong, yet decaying and vulnerable – lay behind his conception. Contemporary politics also lie behind the rather silly ending in which Dionysus, himself now 'tyrant and fascist', becomes a rabble-rousing politician-cum-oracular voice-cum-hippie who proclaims violence, sex in the streets and rebellion against the establishment: 'Take Humphrey's clothes off! Give Mayor Lindsay a total caress! Blow kisses on Lyndon.' Parts of it appear dated today, but it was a serious theatrical experiment in getting performers to open themselves psychologically to a text and parts of Schechner's script and the comments of some of the actors on their experiences are extremely powerful. One Dionysus comments on her own performance, 'I watch the kill, participate sympathetically in it ... I have gone up and away from human needs. I am no longer Joan McIntosh but totally

Dionysus. I feel supreme joy with myself and hatred for everyone in the room. They betrayed me. They didn't give me enough. I was not satisfied.' This does capture one element of a god bent on vengeance, even if it is not the totality of Dionysus or of Euripides' play.

Similar in its focus on a relationship between Dionysus' ambiguous gender and Pentheus' sexuality, is Charles Mee's *Bacchae 2.1* (1993), although Mee uses Euripides' language even less than Schechner does.[20] The contrast between liberalism and conservatism is represented sartorially as Dionysus, in a skirt and five-day growth of beard, is set against Tiresias, Cadmus and Pentheus who are white men in smart suits and ties. The multicultural chorus are revolutionary artists, dressed in flowing bright colours. These Bacchae are not like their ancient counterparts: their rites are unmistakably sexual and they talk of women's initiation rites, genital piercing and tattoos. Mee's Pentheus 'considers himself intellectually superior and charming. His rage and fears are repressed. They come out in the form of wit, sarcasm, scorn, banter, mockery, joking. Only occasionally, in a word or a phrase, is the dark side revealed – and then quickly covered by a smile or some other form of recovery. And only later, when he is more seriously threatened, does the dark side come out fully as dark.' Pentheus contrasts with his two aides who are less inhibited and represent a sexuality only imperfectly covered with the civilised veneer that Pentheus believes that he has perfected. This is a late twentieth-century Pentheus, whose portrayal is clearly influenced by popular psychology, but the distinction he makes between civilised (masculine) pleasures and rough animal (female) pleasures undoubtedly echoes some of the oppositions found in Mee's model.

Modern drama often lays greater emphasis on naturalism than did the ancient theatre, and in accord with this tendency, Mee minimises the more supernatural parts of Euripides' plot. The truth of Dionysus' divinity is left unclear so that he is mostly a symbol of Pentheus' repressed longings. Symbolic interpretations of Dionysus are integral to the critical history of the play (cf. pp. 87-90, 97-100 above), but cannot convey the complexity of a being who is a fully-realised character as well as a symbol. By minimising Dionysus' divinity, Mee is typical of modern adaptors in reworking Euripides' god as a less complex and less ambiguous figure. Mee also portrays Pentheus' horrific death directly on stage rather than through a messenger-speech. His identity is discovered when his wig slips off as Agave strokes his head, whereupon she slams his head into the ground repeatedly in rage at the deceit. The violence is made even more disturbing by the extreme abbreviation of her mad scene. It is never quite clear, as it is in Euripides, that she mutilates her son when under a divine spell, and Mee's minimisation of the supernatural ultimately makes his play more sensational and arguably cruder than its model.

Trends in performance, like those in scholarship, change: even deviant sex and blood can eventually pall. Adaptations and productions of the last couple of decades especially have somewhat downplayed the orgiastic elements of the play in favour of its religious and mythological themes or have used its violence to reflect on contemporary violence.[21] In fact, only a couple of years after *Dionysus in 69*, across the Atlantic, the National Theatre in London staged *The Bacchae of Euripides: A Communion Rite* by Wole Soyinka in 1973. Soyinka's Dionysus is a liberator and avenger of traditionally oppressed groups from a repressive 'priesthood, mercantile princes and other nobility'.[22] Soyinka's portrayal of the god's oppressors may also be a comment on Nigeria's military dictatorship which he had fled.[23] Religious ritual (consisting of mingled African, Greek and Christian elements)[24] is also important in the play and its language incorporates a black gospel idiom, comparable to the language and terminology of Christian prayer which English adaptors sometimes use to convey the religious connotations of Euripides' Greek.[25] As well as a chorus of Bacchantes, the play contains a slave chorus led by a charismatic black figure, akin to a rock star (18).

The play begins as Thebes is preparing its annual scapegoat ritual, in which an old slave is flogged to death to purify the land for the new year. This year, however, in order to prevent a revolt against the horrible custom, but also for his own motives,[26] Tiresias offers himself as a sacrificial victim instead.

He is almost killed but is rescued just in time by Dionysus who then leaves the stage. Although much of his play closely follows Euripides, like many adapters, Soyinka underlines certain elements which are more implicit than explicit in the original, especially in the less than subtle emphasis he lays on Dionysus as representative of the life force (e.g. 19-22.) The humour of the Tiresias and Cadmus scene is also expanded by Soyinka, so that they become a double act who make risqué puns on fawn-skin/foreskin while Cadmus complains that he cannot get his collapsible thyrsus to stay erect.[27] Soyinka's Pentheus is a tyrant with no mitigating features and Soyinka, like many other adaptors and even some scholars, attributes his authoritarianism to a refusal to recognise the Dionysiac in his own nature. Soyinka reworks the Euripidean earthquake and destruction of the palace as a splendid duet between a Bacchante and the slave chorus as they chant for its destruction (52-3) until Dionysus is finally revealed, standing in flames around his mother's grave.

The following scene with Pentheus, the herdsman and Dionysus runs largely along Euripidean lines, until (65-6) Dionysus spells out to Pentheus what at most is implied by Euripides – his love of chains and iron which, he says, 'has replaced your umbilical cord'. The god touches Pentheus on his navel and turns him round and round: he is hypnotised and then shown 'the future' of the cult in the form of two wedding scenes performed as silent plays within the play. The first suggests that there is a wild fawnskin-covered Bacchante in even the most decorous groom,[28] while in the other, a figure wearing a crown of Christ-like thorns and Dionysiac ivy presides over a mingled version of the stories of Martha and Mary and the miracle of the changing of water into wine at Cana (66-9). Once he has seen this, Pentheus expresses a longing to drink and go to the mountains with Dionysus. Though he insists on wearing armour, Dionysus dresses him as a woman anyway and he is too senseless to realise it. Once Pentheus and Dionysus have left the stage, some of the slave chorus join with the Bacchae to throw off Pentheus' kingship and, accompanied by an expanded version of the equivalent

Euripidean choral song at this point, they mime a hunt and capture of Pentheus. Just as they are about to strike the death blow, a messenger appears, and the sequence of his speech, Agave's arrival and the revelation of what she has done follows the Euripidean pattern closely. Tiresias, however, has remained on stage and explains to an uncomprehending Cadmus that the old ritual was mere cruelty without the power to cleanse the land, and only Pentheus' death could renew Thebes (96-7).

For Soyinka, Euripides' play deserved 'a more fitting ending' (x) and he turns Pentheus' dismemberment into a spiritual blessing for his community. The severed head begins to spurt a red liquid: it is found to be wine and the play ends in communal drinking. Soyinka's emphasis on the removal of the tyrant and the creation of a ritual of unity for the Theban community attempts to make Pentheus' violent death less problematic than it is in Euripides' *Bacchae*. Indeed, his ending recalls the readings of Seaford and those who believe that the play ultimately affirms the primacy of the democratic community over the individual and the royal house.[29] But just as these readings may be too optimistic in what they ignore, so Soyinka's reworking of the play is problematic in its refusal to explain Agave's suffering: unlike her Euripidean counterpart, she had never spoken against Dionysus, and yet she is still the instrument of her son's death. She accepts her son's murder with merely minimal protest and almost immediately accepts a drink of his blood: the incestuous and cannibalistic image is distinctly unpleasant. The ending of this play, which ranks her suffering as insignificant compared with the unity of the city and Soyinka's 'tumultous [sic] celebration of life' (ix) has therefore often been found unsatisfactory.[30] Soyinka's one-dimensionally evil Pentheus tips the balance of the play very much in favour of Dionysus who loses much of his darkness and comes simply – even simplistically – to represent the importance of a balanced life. Modern adaptations often make Pentheus' position entirely unreasonable and Dionysus correspondingly more admirable, losing much of the ambiguity in Euripides' portrayal of the two opponents. Kenneth Cavander even mistranslates *Bacchae* 881 ('What is good is always dear') as 'Balance is all'.[31]

The Japanese director Suzuki Tadashi has long been fascinated by the *Bacchae* and has in his repertoire several versions
of the play, the best known of which is the bilingual version
produced in 1981 in Japan and the United States.[32] He too sets
the play in a multicultural framework, while also stressing its
metatheatrical and dualistic elements. Pentheus, Cadmus and
Tiresias are English-speaking while Dionysus is Japanese: the
messenger and the Chorus alternate between Japanese and
English. The technique is especially effective in scenes which
emphasise the communication gap between Pentheus and
Dionysus. Suzuki makes a play within a play which begins with
the last words of the *Bacchae* translated into Japanese as a
prelude to a performance of Euripides' *Bacchae* by a group of
people who are oppressed by a tyrannical ruler and seek liberation through their performance. The people identify with
Dionysus and are pleased at Pentheus' murder, but afterwards,
as Agave and Cadmus revert to their pre-play personae and sit
drinking tea, a resurrected Pentheus returns, reciting his
opening lines, and murders them. Suzuki illustrates an eternal
cycle of miscommunication, oppression and revenge in which
roles change, but the same power structures exist and no one
learns anything. Although Suzuki's *Bacchae* is as long as
Euripides', there is less text, since Suzuki often conveys
meaning through gestures and silence rather than language. As
in Greek drama, violence is not directly shown, but is represented symbolically or by gesture.

The play has a clearly political dimension. A clash of East
and West is played out in the opposition of Dionysus, who
commands his worshippers with a silent authority, and
Pentheus, who rules with violence and obsessive reliance on
the laws. Western racism is also demonstrated by Pentheus'
refusal to understand Dionysus' Japanese. Like Soyinka,
Suzuki creates a relatively benevolent Dionysus, who symbolises the longings of the oppressed, while Pentheus represents
their oppressors. Even so, Dionysus no less than Pentheus
represents nationalism and imperialism: the absolute obedience shown to him by his followers is unsettling and
reminiscent of the absolute obedience shown, for example, by

the kamikaze pilots in the Second World War. At one point, the movements of Dionysus' followers even resemble the Bunraku tradition of puppet theatre in Japan, and by portraying their conformism so strikingly, it is clear that Suzuki intends to condemn more than the Western imperialism represented by Pentheus.

The *Bacchae* has had a number of operatic settings such as Egon Wellesz's *Die Bakhantinnen* (1931) and G.F. Ghedini's *Le Baccanti* (1948). The libretto for Hans Werner Henze's *The Bassarids* (1966) was written by W.H. Auden and Chester Kallman, who emphasise Dionysus' sinister aspect. Through the ascetic Pentheus' repression both of his instincts and of his people, they focus on the conflict between repression and liberation which is common in modern reworkings of the play. Each side is characterised by different music – Dionysus in dance rhythm, Pentheus in march-time – until at the climax Pentheus' music is absorbed by that of Dionysus. John Buller wrote his 1992 opera *Bakxai*, sung in Greek and some English, and incorporating some fragments of ancient Greek melody, partly as a reaction to Kallman and Auden's text. Roy Travis's *Black Bacchants* (1982), in a parallel to Wole Soyinka's play, includes traditional West African dance rhythms and instruments. The most recent operatic version of the *Bacchae*, *Die Heimkehr des Dionysos* ('The Homecoming of Dionysus'), a free adaptation in which Agave has no part and Pentheus commits suicide through failing to accept the Dionysus in himself, was written in the 1930s and preserved in the papers of Edwin Geist after he was shot by the Nazis in Lithuania. His opera was finally performed there in 2002.[33]

Harry Partch's opera *Revelation in the Courthouse Park* (1960-1) is a double narrative which alternates between an abbreviated version of the ancient text and a modern retelling in a small mid-Western 1950s town. The god Dionysus is paired with a charismatic rock star named Dion (a symbol of 'dominant mediocrity' according to Partch) while Pentheus becomes Sonny, a 'lost soul' who is a more isolated and pitiable figure than Pentheus. Agave is Mom, Dion's chief groupie. Partch saw similarities between the ecstatic religion of Euripides' play and the mingling of sexual and religious feeling at rock concerts and at charismatic religious gatherings in America: he therefore reworks Euripides' choral passages in the style of American religious revival meetings. His attitude to these religious and sexual phenomena resembles that of Winnington Ingram: the women threaten 'degradation and annihilation for anyone unwilling to praise or at least respect their particular pattern of mediocrity and conformity'.[34] The opera ends as Agave screams 'Noooo!' when she realises what she is holding in her hands. Partch's music relies on his own handmade instruments, some of which are inspired by Greek models, and his orchestration characterises Bacchic ecstasy through sounds of piercing wind instruments, percussion and repeated rhythmical chanting. *A Refined Look at Existence* (1968) by the Australian writer Rodney Milgate also portrays Dionysus (here Donny) as a rock star and quasi-religious figure who inspires devotion in his fans, while his opponent becomes Penthouse Champion, the half-Aborigine son of Igave Champion. Milgate recreates the whole house of Cadmus as a dysfunctional Australian family in a play whose mixture of kitchen-sink drama and philosophical speculation is jarring.

To portray Dionysus as a rock star deprives the god of much of his complexity, but this has been one of his most popular incarnations since the first great age of rock music in the 1960s, for his allure and apparent decadence and for the mixture of masculine and feminine which Euripides emphasises in the god and which is retained by archetypal stars such as Mick Jagger.[35] Like experimental productions which emphasise audience participation, such interpretations bring us in some ways close to an experience of Dionysiac ecstasy, while being less successful at rendering Euripides' *Bacchae* as a literary text with its own specific historical and cultural context. The 1990s saw the growth of 'rave culture' which, in its emphasis on community, loud music, dancing and drugs is analogous to the Bacchic experience in the same diminished, but not insignificant, way that rock stars are analogues of the god himself. *Dionysus/Diotekk* was Robin Bond's attempt – strongly influenced by *Dionysus in 69* – to reproduce in a modern environment some of the effects of Bacchic ritual through a rave-influenced production in a New Zealand nightclub. After the formal performance, audience and performers mingled on the dance floor into the small hours with strobes, lasers and occasional snatches of Bond's translation of Euripides. Bond himself considers his version successful in conveying something of the (conjectured) atmosphere of Bacchic ritual, but less so in conveying Euripides' text to those unfamiliar with the play.[36]

Even before the age of multimedia which allows for technical effects only dreamed of by Artaud (n. 18 above), various 'special effects' proved irresistible to some directors: in one late 1960s production, a live snake twisted in Dionysus' hands as he spoke his final speech, while more recently (1987), in a Venezuelan production, described by its reviewer as a 'flamenco Passion play', a live hound sat on the stage awaiting Pentheus' death and was eventually rewarded with a (presumably simulated) dinner of human flesh. A 1987 production at the Guthrie Theater is most famous for the impressive collapse of Pentheus' palace.[37] Currently, hi-tech productions of the play are fashionable. *Trance Bacchae* (1997) comprises 'a bunch of high class musicians, VJs, performers, actors, programmers which perform live for about 7 hours.' Greek text of the *Bacchae* is sampled and mingled with a multilingual text and music inspired by Greek, Arab and Jewish traditions and broadcast around the performance space, described as 'an immersive sound and video environment'. Its creators claim to combine theatre with rave and to eradicate the distinction between performers and public – in itself a Dionysiac notion (Euripides *Bacchae* 206-7).[38] In *Bakkee* by the experimental group Madlab[39] the audience follows the characters through a labyrinth whose rooms provide a surround-sound and vision experience intended to eradicate audience passivity. This version is also notable for a relatively even-handed treatment of Dionysus and Pentheus. The play is set in a dystopian, violent future in which Pentheus rules his masses by manipulating them into zombie-like placidity through drugs and the media: although his policy has stemmed the violence, it has not created true happiness. He is challenged by the cult-leader Dionysus who condemns this drug-addled existence but advocates instead the use of extreme ritual violence in order to demystify violence and strip it of its power. Though futuristic, the production is quite conventional in its reading of the play as a conflict between acquiescence to oppression versus individualism. With a somewhat similar focus, a production by the York-based Actors of Dionysus (2000) compared Dionysus' threat to Theban society with the threats to society made by modern cults such as the Branch Davidians at Waco (1993) or Aum Shinrikyo (1995) in Japan.

Even more of a contrast to the standard condemnation of Pentheus and sanitisation of Dionysus comes in John Bowen's *The Disorderly Women* (1969), a story, according to its author, in which 'a good man ... is destroyed by ... his denial both in himself and others of what is instinctive, irrational'.[40] This Pentheus is a pinstriped bureaucrat who has devoted his life to creating a land of 'Everything in moderation. Everything works ... not exciting, but it *is* noble.' (52-3). The women of Thebes are bored by this soulless utopia and are easily lured by Dionysus, a hippie who presides over services of mutual worship between himself and the Bacchantes: he is not the imperious god of Euripides, except at the end of the play. The miracles of Bacchic worship are portrayed as the results of LSD and one powerful scene shows its gradual effects on the women as they proclaim the dullness of their lives in Thebes before Dionysus' advent, in a sort of revival meeting complete with cries of 'Testify!' Pentheus does his best to understand the cult since he is essentially a humanist and values free religious expression: closer to Euripides' Pentheus is his Permanent Private Secretary who vigorously condemns it. Even Pentheus' eventual arrival in women's clothes at Cithaeron results from better motives than those of Euripides' Pentheus: originally he intends to send someone else, but when faced with accusations of endangering a subordinate, he shoulders the responsibility fitting for a leader. Bowen portrays Pentheus' murder in an intense scene as he is surrounded by women who at first tease him verbally, as though they were children on a playground, but the teasing increasingly becomes aggressive and physical until it climaxes in murder. Overall, the play is an uneven mixture of modern realism, comedy and some scenes, such as the last scene of Agave's madness, which closely resemble Euripides.

What is 'authentic performance' of Greek drama? This is a particularly important issue for the *Bacchae* because many of its themes seem so modern. Is authenticity an attempt to reproduce the practices of the ancient Greek theatre, which will make the experience somewhat alien for a modern audience, or is there a kind of equivalent authenticity of experience for a modern audience which will conform less closely to ancient Greek stage conventions?[41] As we have seen, many productions of the last few decades have espoused the latter approach in various ways, but it remains to mention two somewhat different recent performances. Sir Peter Hall's 2002 production retained the use of masks, three actors and a chorus of 15 in a traditional reading of the play in which Pentheus is characterised by a mixture of callowness, vulnerability and fascism. Hall emphasised the standard oppositions of emotion and reason, male and female and so on: he also emphasised the play's metatheatrical dimension, especially in its use of masks.[42] Most firm in their repudiation of the naturalistic acting and updating which have dominated modern productions of the *Bacchae* are the Thiasos Theatre Company, for whom ancient drama demands a non-naturalistic, highly formalistic style and any attempt at modernising is 'grim, dreary and self-indulgent'.[43] Their *Bacchae* was performed in London in 2003 with a translation by Richard Seaford which reverted to Greek at heightened moments, such as the destruction of Pentheus' palace, 'so that our audience could enjoy the musicality of the language'. This *Bacchae* emphasises the tragedy's religious elements and the centrality of the chorus, whose importance is often minimised in modern productions. Such a performance, claims a reviewer, 'alienates at the same time as it strikes chords of recognition. It eschews straightforward interpretation and glib jokes about drunken frenzy.'[44]

Hangovers

Because of the multiple symbolic possibilities generated by the conflict between Pentheus and Dionysus – control and liberty, man and god, man and woman and so on[45] – many cultural productions either explore these conflicts but detach them from characters called Dionysus and Pentheus, or seem otherwise coloured by elements of the plot or imagery of the *Bacchae*, without being classifiable as adaptations of Euripides.[46] As such, they lie beyond the scope of this book, but a few examples will typify the huge variety of Dionysiac or Euripidean motifs in modern literature, film or opera. Karol Szymanowski's opera *Krol Roger* (1926) is set in medieval Sicily but is often classified as an adaptation of the *Bacchae*. King Roger at first resists the allure of the charismatic Shepherd for whom queen and courtiers have deserted him, but is finally reconciled to the force he represents: the opera commends a primal paganism which brings new life through the triumph of irrationality. Hints of the *Bacchae* have been seen in Pasolini's film *Teorema* in which a stranger comes to a household and arouses erotic desires in the whole household: these cause the dissolution of the bourgeois family but occasion the retreat of their peasant maid to her birthplace and eventual transformation into a saint. For Hans Oranje, this plot recalls the contrast between the disaster which Cadmus' dishonest 'common sense' acceptance of Dionysus as a family member causes and the religious intuition which leads the shepherd on Cithaeron fully to accept the god.[47]

Like *Dionysus in 69*, David Lan and Caryl Churchill's *A Mouthful of Birds* (1986) originated from a series of dramatic workshops. It focusses on the themes of 'possession and women being violent', through their idiosyncratic interpretation of the *Bacchae* as a play about 'the pleasure of physical power, the exhilaration of destruction, and finally a recognition of its horror'. Central to this play is the idea of the 'undefended day' in which its characters are at the mercy of violent forces inside and outside them. Through numerous short dialogues, Lan and Churchill portray seven people who are each possessed by something (addiction, anxiety, passion and so on). Dionysus (a man in a white petticoat) appears sporadically as a malign presence, and into a modern context Lan and Churchill incorporate Euripidean motifs, such as gender ambiguity, infanticide, the dressing of a Pentheus figure as a woman and his murder at the climax of the play. Similar in its reading of the *Bacchae* in terms of female empowerment through violence is Maureen Duffy's play *Rites* (1969), described by Duffy as 'Agave's story'. Very much of its time in its intense emphasis on the damage inflicted on women by a hostile society, it focusses on a group of socially and economically powerless women who meet in a public toilet to perform daily rituals of personal grooming. Gradually, they form a solidarity with one another which emboldens them to kill a figure of ambiguous gender whom they believe to be a male spy, but who turns out to be a woman. They band together to throw the body into the incinerator and depart in a conspiratorial silence. Duffy, like John Bowen in the same year, wrote in order to offer actresses more interesting roles at a time when they had long been stuck 'at the loom' (*Bacchae* 1236), as it were, with few opportunities to transcend stereotypically female roles in the theatre.[48]

Donna Tartt's best-selling novel, *The Secret History* (New York: Knopff, 1992) in which a group of Classics majors commit murder in the course of attempting to recreate a Dionysiac ritual, has little direct relationship with the *Bacchae* but is connected with it thematically – particularly in its portrayal of a destructive Dionysiac spirituality – and, as reviewers have noted, partly resembles a tragedy in being structured around a violent crime and its aftermath. The Bacchae have even surfaced in popular television in an episode of *Xena: Warrior Princess*. Here, the Bacchae are vampires and Bacchus a physically intimidating individual, who resembles traditional portrayals of the devil. He is easily outwitted by Xena to offer a message of female empowerment far less equivocal than anything Euripides offers.

This swift tour through post-Euripidean versions of the *Bacchae* is far from complete, but it does offer some indication of the astonishing vigour of Euripides' play. In the power and abundance of its later forms, it is a piece of work that truly exemplifies Euripides' conception of Dionysus' own power to offer remarkable and numerous gifts.

Notes

For secondary literature whose full title is not given in the notes, see the Guide to Further Reading at the end of the book, where the abbreviated title is keyed to its full form.

1. Euripides and the Theatre

1. See R.P. Winnington Ingram, 'Euripides: *Poietes Sophos*', reprinted in J. Mossman (editor), *Oxford Readings in Classical Studies: Euripides* (Oxford: Oxford University Press, 2003), pp. 47-63.

2. The distinction between the Dionysian (characterised by wildness, spontaneity and emotion) and the Apollonian (characterised by reason and control) was most famously conceptualised in the nineteenth century by Friedrich Nietzsche in *The Birth of Tragedy* (Leipzig: E.W. Fritzsch, 1872): see pp. 81-3.

3. For the problems of credibility in ancient biography, see M. Lefkowitz, *Lives of the Greek Poets* (Baltimore: Johns Hopkins University Press, 1981), pp. 88-105, whose position on nearly all the ancient traditions surrounding Euripides is sceptical.

4. Along with these two plays, 17 others out of the 92 traditionally ascribed to Euripides have been transmitted to the modern world.

5. P.T. Stevens, 'Euripides and the Athenians', *Journal of Hellenic Studies* 76 (1956), pp. 87-94. The Sophocles anecdote appears in Satyros' *Life of Euripides*, 45.

6. Indeed, for Aristophanes, a comic playwright and Euripides' contemporary, the purpose of tragedy was to 'make men better' (*Frogs* 1009). The context is comic, but few in Athens would have denied that tragedy offered moral and educational food for thought as well as entertainment and emotional release for its audience.

7. Segal, *Dionysiac Poetics*, pp. 14-15; see also Sourvinou-Inwood, *Tragedy and Athenian Religion*, pp. 19-23. On Phrynichus and the issues raised by his story, see D. Rosenbloom, 'Shouting "Fire" in a Crowded Theatre: Phrynichus' Capture of Miletos and the Politics of Fear in Early Attic Tragedy', *Philologus* 137 (1993), pp. 159-96.

8. Aristophanes was Euripides' most famous ancient critic and found his style and themes a reliable source of humour throughout his own career. His *Frogs* (405 BCE) stages a contest between Euripides and Aeschylus in the underworld in which Euripides is criticised for verbosity and intellectual nit-picking (954-70, 1078-80) and for excessive realism in the portrayal of immoral women (1052-3). In his own defence, Euripides claims that he has made tragedy more democratic by expanding its traditional cast of kings and heroes to include humbler characters such as women and slaves (*Frogs* 952-4). Euripides was also notorious for dressing his beggar king Telephus in rags, rather than the traditional grand costume of a tragic actor: Aristophanes *Acharnians* 415, 430-2. For a useful summary of the complaints Euripides typically attracts from modern critics, see D. Kovacs, *The Heroic Muse: Studies in the Hippolytus and Hecuba of Euripides* (Baltimore: Johns Hopkins University Press, 1987), pp. 1-21.

9. M.R. Lefkowitz, '"Impiety" and "Atheism"', in Euripides' Dramas', *Classical Quarterly* 39 (1989), pp. 70-82. For the charges, see for example, Aristophanes *Thesmophoriazousae* 450f. and G.W. Bond, *Euripides: Heracles* (Oxford: Clarendon Press, 1988), pp. 399-400. Sourvinou-Inwood, *Tragedy and Athenian Religion*, pp. 31, 294-300, disputes Euripides' alleged religious unorthodoxy, but his contemporaries do seem to have distinguished between Euripides' religious attitudes and those of his predecessors.

10. G. Devereux, 'The Psychotherapy Scene in Euripides' *Bacchae*', *Journal of Hellenic Studies* 90 (1970), pp. 35-48.

11. Grube, *Drama of Euripides*, p. 398 calls it 'as near technical perfection as any other extant tragedy'.

12. A sentiment from the funeral oration attributed to Pericles by Thucydides, 2.45.2.

13. R. Just, *Women in Athenian Law and Life* (London: Routledge, 1989), pp. 106-21; D. Cohen, 'Seclusion, Separation and the Status of Women', *Greece and Rome* 36 (1989), pp. 3-15.

14. For a fascinating account of women and Greek religion, see now Goff, *Citizen Bacchae*.

15. In favour of the presence of women: J. Henderson, 'Women and the Athenian Dramatic Festivals', *Transactions of the American Philological Society* 121 (1991), pp. 133-47. S. Goldhill, 'Representing Democracy: Women at the Great Dionysia', in *Ritual, Finance, Politics: Democratic Accounts Presented to David Lewis* (Oxford: Clarendon Press, 1994), pp. 347-69, offers some challenges to his arguments.

16. Ritually, women are associated with both birth and death, with the body at its most vulnerable and inelegant: Goff, *Citizen Bacchae*, pp. 3-4, 35-6.

17. For the fear inspired by what untamed nature can do to a man adrift from civilisation, compare Sophocles *Philoctetes* 952-7. The assimilation of women to animals ('cow' and so on) is not new: the seventh-century satirist Semonides categorises women as animals according to their (mostly unflattering) characteristics. Thus the Pig Woman is dirty (7.1-6), the Monkey Woman annoying and untrustworthy (7.70-83).

18. R. Padel, 'Women: Model for Possession by Greek Daemons', in A. Cameron and A. Kuhrt (editors), *Images of Women in Antiquity* (Detroit: Wayne State Press, 1983), pp. 3-19.

19. R. Just, *Women in Athenian Law and Life* (London: Routledge, 1989), pp.161-93.

20. The Pythagorean Table of Opposites (in Aristotle *Metaphysics* 986a15) opposes limit, unity, male, straight, light and good to the unlimited, plurality, female, crooked, dark, and evil. A good account of these polarities is offered by P. Cartledge, *The Greeks: A Portrait of Self and Others* (Oxford and New York: Oxford University Press, 1993), esp. pp. 8-17.

21. For a classic treatment of non-Greeks in tragedy, see E. Hall, *Inventing the Barbarian* (Oxford: Clarendon Press, 1989), esp. pp. 1-17.

22. E. Hall, 'The Sociology of Athenian Tragedy', in Easterling, *Companion*, pp. 93-127 (118).

23. Euripides' ambivalent representation is analogous to the social function of the Dionysus-cult discussed by F. Zeitlin, 'Cultic Models of the Female: Rites of Dionysus and Demeter', *Arethusa* 15 (1982), pp. 129-57 (130-4). By Zeitlin's interpretation, on the one hand women's participation in the cult of Dionysus is a liberation from their normal role of confinement in the house under male control; yet simultaneously the wildness that this cult temporarily allows them is itself a confirmation of an innately dangerous disposition which necessitates the norms of male control.

24. Pickard-Cambridge, *Dramatic Festivals*, is a fundamental source for the ancient evidence, although E. Csapo and W.J. Slater, *The Context of Ancient Drama* (Ann Arbor: University of Michigan Press, 1995) is a more user-friendly reference work. Other helpful treatments include Taplin, *Greek Tragedy*; R. Rehm, *Greek Tragic Theatre* (London: Routledge, 1992); D. Wiles, *Greek Theatre Performance: An Introduction* (Cambridge: Cambridge University Press, 2000), 89-164; J. Michael Walton, *Greek Theatre Practice* (Greenwood Press, CT, 1980). Easterling, *Companion*, pp. 3-90, contains several very helpful essays. For an interesting if necessarily speculative account of the development of the Dionysia, see C. Sourvinou-Inwood, *Tragedy and Athenian Religion*, pp. 67-140.

25. A kind of burlesque of some of the myths of the preceding tragedies, performed by actors wearing tragic dress and a chorus dressed as satyrs, companions of Dionysus. Aristotle (*Poetics*, 1449a20) states that tragedy developed from satyr play rather than the other way round.

26. On the *chorêgoi*, see Peter Wilson, *The Athenian Institution of the Khoregia: The Chorus, the City and the Stage* (Cambridge: Cambridge University Press, 2000).

27. Isocrates, *On the Peace*, 82. See Goldhill, 'The Great Dionysia', pp. 99-106.

28. Of course tragedy is not merely the utilitarian, propagandistic genre that this emphasis on its political dimension may suggest, and some recent scholarship has questioned the current emphasis on its presumed political functions: see J. Griffin, 'The Social Function of Attic Tragedy', *Classical Quarterly* 48 (1998), pp. 39-61, with the rejoinder by S. Goldhill, 'Civic Ideology and the Problem of Difference: The Politics of Aeschylean Tragedy Once Again', *Journal of Hellenic Studies* 120 (2000), pp. 34-56. The two approaches are not irreconcilable, provided that the impact of the aesthetic pleasures of tragedy on its audience is fully acknowledged and 'political' is interpreted broadly enough to include questions of how to live in a world of anxiety and suffering.

29. On religion in comedy, see C. Sourvinou-Inwood, *Tragedy and Athenian Religion*, p. 53.

30. On how literary genre can affect our interpretation of Greek religion, see R. Parker, 'Gods Cruel and Kind: Tragic and Civic Theology', in C. Pelling (editor), *Greek Tragedy and the Historian* (Oxford: Clarendon Press, 1997), pp. 143-160.

31. J. Mikalson, *Honor Thy Gods: Popular Religion in Greek Tragedy* (Chapel Hill, NC: University of North Carolina Press, 1991), pp. 1-16 and 203-36: C. Sourvinou-Inwood, 'Tragedy and Religion: Constructs and Readings', in C. Pelling (editor), *Greek Tragedy and the Historian* (Oxford: Clarendon Press, 1997), pp. 161-86 and *Tragedy and Athenian Religion*, esp. pp. 19-21, 31, 49, 177, 243, 331, 416.

32. Xenophanes 10 blames Homer and Hesiod for creating gods lacking in common morality; Plato (e.g. *Republic* 383b) bans poets from his ideal state, partly because they tell lies about the gods; Cadmus in Euripides' *Bacchae* vainly complains that gods should be better at restraining their anger than Dionysus has been (*Bacchae* 1348; cf. Euripides *Hippolytus* 120; *Heracles* 1341-6).

33. Goff, *Citizen Bacchae*, p. 13; C. Sourvinou-Inwood, *Tragedy and Athenian Religion*, p, 20.

34. See K. Dover, *Aristophanes: Frogs*, (Oxford: Clarendon Press, 1993), p. 41.

35. D. Wiles, 'The Use of Masks in Modern Performances of Greek Drama', in *Dionysus Since 69*, pp. 245-63. See also Chapter 5.

36. Taplin, *Greek Tragedy*, p. 119-20, but some scholars, uneasy at a contrast between the Chorus' description of significant damage to the palace (591-2) and its total absence on stage prefer different solutions: for a summary of approaches and a more theoretical discussion of the issues, see S. Goldhill, *Reading Greek Tragedy* (Cambridge: Cambridge University Press, 1986), pp. 277-84.

37. It is one of only four plays of Euripides which are structured around the classic sequence of prologue, *parodos*, five episodes and *exodos*: C. Collard, *Euripides: Greece and Rome New Surveys in the Classics* 14 (Oxford: Clarendon Press, 1981), p. 15. Dodds, *Commentary*, p. xxxvi.

38. A twelve-syllable line, divided into three groups of four, of which the first syllable can be long or short, with the remaining three syllables in the order long-short-long. Thus: x– ∪– | x– ∪– | x– ∪–. Variants are possible.

39. Ionics (∪∪– –): E. Hall, *Inventing the Barbarian* (Oxford: Clarendon Press, 1989), pp. 82-3; trochaic tetrameter catalectic (– ∪x∪| – ∪x∪| – ∪x∪| – ∪–): Dodds p. 152.

40. C. Segal, 'Chorus and Community in Euripides' *Bacchae*', in L. Edmunds and R. Wallace (editors), *Poet, Public and Performance: Ancient Genres* (Baltimore: Johns Hopkins University Press, 1997), pp. 65-86.

2. Dionysus and Athens

1. Henrichs, 'Greek Maenadism', p. 122; 'Loss of Self', p. 229.

2. Versnel, *Ter Unus*, p. 135; D. Obbink, 'Dionysos Poured Out: Ancient and Modern Theories of Sacrifice and Cultural Formation', in *Masks*, pp. 65-86 (69).

3. Bremmer, 'Greek Maenadism Reconsidered'.

4. Henrichs, *OCD*, p. 482; Burkert, *Greek Religion*, p. 162.

5. Burkert, *Greek Religion*, pp. 31, 162; Otto, *Dionysus*, p.53; Henrichs, *OCD*, p. 479.

6. Detienne, *Dionysos at Large*, p. 5. As Other, he is associated with the East, the home of the Persians, the quintessential Others, and in fifth-century Athens he is even partially assimilated to Sabazius, an Eastern god, whose worship, like that of Dionysus in the *Bacchae*, included ecstatic nocturnal rites, fawnskin clothing and snake-handling. Sabazius is the son of the Great Mother Cybele who is herself assimilated to Rhea, the mother of Zeus and Dionysus himself in Cretan myth: Dodds, *Commentary*, pp. xxiii-v, 76-7. The similarities between one ecstatic cult and another tend to blur the lines between the gods whom they honour.

7. Homer describes Dionysus as 'mad'. The god who maddens is easily characterised as mad himself: Otto, *Dionysus,* p. 54.

8. This detail is common in Bacchic myth and may reflect the historical organisation of maenadic cult at Thebes which comprised three bands of Maenads: Henrichs, 'Greek Maenadism', p. 137.

Notes to pages 24-26

9. Antonius Liberalis *Metamorphoses* 10; Aelian *Historical Miscellany* 3.42; Plutarch *Moralia* 299e-300a.

10. The scene is portrayed on a famous cup (ABV 146, 21) by Exekias, *c*.540-30.

11. On Dionysus as wine-god, see Leinieks, *City of Dionysos*, pp. 179-93, but Dionysus' primary connection with wine is not universally accepted (Burkert, *Greek Religion*, p. 162) and even if the connection with wine is fundamental to understanding him it is vital to remember that Greek religious thought depends on a process of symbolism and analogy whereby frothing wine can be conceptualised as belonging in the same category as blood or sap or sperm or the moistness associated with procreation: Plutarch *Moralia* 365a. By such multiple analogies, the significance of Dionysus is broadened beyond wine to become a god who represents the life force in a very broad sense: Otto, *Dionysus*, pp. 156-7; Detienne, *Dionysos at Large*, pp. 56-64; L. Farnell, *Cults of the Greek States* V (Oxford: Clarendon Press, 1909), pp. 95-123; Oranje, *Euripides' Bacchae*, p. 102.

12. Detienne, *Dionysos at Large,* pp. 33-5.

13. Cf. Hesiod *Works and Days* 614; one of Dionysus' cult titles is 'Liberator': Plutarch *Moralia* 613c, 680b, 716b; Otto, *Dionysus*, p. 134ff.

14. Segal, *Dionysiac Poetics*, p. 15.

15. ['E]veryone who surrenders to this god must risk abandoning his everyday identity and becoming mad; this is both divine and wholesome:' Burkert, *Greek Religion*, p. 162.

16. Archilochus 77D; cf. also Alcaeus 129 and Anacreon 357.

17. Herodotus 5.67.5, cf. 1.23 which attributes the invention of the dithyramb to Arion of Corinth in the last quarter of the seventh century. This is not literally true but may be another indication of Corinthian interest in Dionysus at this time. See also Seaford, *Reciprocity*, pp. 327-9.

18. Burkert, *Greek Religion*, p. 290.

19. Henrichs, *OCD*, pp. 480-1; M. Jameson, 'The Asexuality of Dionysus', in *Masks*, pp. 44-64. Particularly at the end of the *Bacchae*, Euripides' Dionysus is characterised by detachment and indifference to human suffering.

20. M. Jameson, 'The Asexuality of Dionysus', in *Masks*, pp. 44-64 (62-3); Seaford, *Reciprocity*, pp. 237, 246.

21. Henrichs, 'He Has a God', p. 23 makes a more absolute distinction between the two incarnations of Dionysus.

22. Cf. *Masks*, p. 2. Sicyon: Pausanias 2.7.5-6; cf. Euripides *Bacchae* 861; Lesbos: Alcaeus 29; Naxos: *F GrH* 499 F 4.

23. Henrichs, 'Loss of Self', p. 235, n. 85. On Orphic matters, see also below.

24. Herodotus 2.146.2: Otto, *Dionysus*, p. 73.

25. Henrichs, 'Greek Maenadism', p. 133, n. 40. Rites of Dionysus in which both sexes played a part include the Great Dionysia at Athens and many other local festivals in Greece.

26. Otto, *Dionysus*, p. 134; Detienne, *Dionysos at Large*, pp. 20-1.

27. D. Obbink, 'Dionysos Poured Out: Ancient and Modern Theories of Sacrifice and Cultural Formation', in *Masks*, pp. 65-86 (76); Henrichs, 'Greek Maenadism', pp. 124, 148-52; Bremmer, 'Greek Maenadism Reconsidered', pp. 274-7.

28. Cf. Bremmer, 'Greek Maenadism Reconsidered', pp. 286-7.

29. Cf. Seaford, *Reciprocity*, pp. 258-9. Temporary inversion of normality is particularly common in initiation ritual whereby adolescents, in order to become part of the adult community, must experience a time outside the community before they can be reintegrated into it. Thus young men will wear women's clothes (and vice versa) and live on the borders of the city for a prescribed period before returning to take up their proper social role as adults.

30. Obbink, 'Dionysos Poured Out: Ancient and Modern Theories of Sacrifice and Cultural Formation', in *Masks*, pp. 65-86 (69); Seaford, *Reciprocity,* p. 259f.

31. Obbink, p. 75; Bremmer, 'Greek Maenadism Reconsidered', pp. 151-2. Older scholarship, such as Dodds, *The Greeks and the Irrational* (Berkeley, CA: University of California Press, 1951), p. 277, imagined the *ômophagia* as a sacramental consumption of Dionysus – to be like a god, eat a god – but more recent scholars are sceptical. Consumption of the body is, in fact, strongly rejected in the *Bacchae*.

32. See also the discussions of Maenadism by Goff, *Citizen Bacchae*, pp. 16, 83, 136, 272-9, who compares it with the phenomenon of possession by a spirit in some modern cultures, as a means of claiming a measure of independence from, and even exerting aggression on, the dominant members of society by those who have been marginalised.

33. The torches and drums may represent the thunder and lightning which is associated with Dionysus (cf. *Bacchae* 594-9). These represent both the epiphany of the god and are also important in initiations into mystery cults: Seaford, *Commentary*, pp. 195-8 and see below.

34. Bremmer, 'Greek Maenadism Reconsidered', pp. 278-83.

35. Cf. Henrichs, 'Greek Maenadism', p. 135; Burkert, *Greek Religion*, pp. 291-2.

36. P.E. Easterling, 'A Show for Dionysus', p. 45.

37. See H. Parke, *Festivals of the Athenians* (Ithaca, 1977), pp. 104-6; Pickard Cambridge, *Dramatic Festivals*, pp. 25-42.

38. Versnel, *Ter Unus,* pp. 146-7; Pickard Cambridge, *Dramatic Festivals*, p. 32f.

39. Pickard Cambridge, *Dramatic Festivals*, pp. 1-25; Burkert,

Greek Religion, pp. 165-6, 237-42; Detienne, *Dionysos at Large*, pp. 38-9; Parke, *Festivals of the Athenians* (Ithaca, 1977), pp. 107-20.

40. Cf. p. 31. After Erigone hanged herself, the young women of Athens started to follow suit until her ghost was appeased by the establishment of the *aiôra*. The meaning of the ritual is unclear. Perhaps it was expiation for death of an innocent victim, or to promote fertility, or even to protect vulnerable young girls from similar self-harm: see J. Neils and J. Oakley, *Coming of Age in Classical Athens: Images of Childhood from the Classical Past* (New Haven and London: Yale University Press, 2003), pp. 145-9 with references.

41. The City Dionysia brought the people of Attica together in one place whereas the Rural Dionysia was celebrated in diverse locations and in diverse ways over the region. It took place in December and in some parts of Attica included dramatic performances: Pickard Cambridge, *Dramatic Festivals*, pp. 42-54.

42. Pausanias 1.38.9. Eleutherae came under Athenian jurisdiction in the second half of the sixth century, which may be a *terminus post quem* for the beginning or expansion of the Great Dionysia. The Greek root 'eleuther-' means 'free'. Dionysus Eleuthereus is 'Dionysus of Eleutherae' and 'Dionysus the Liberator': perhaps his patronage of the festival was connected with the establishment of democracy (and freedom from the tyrants) at the very end of the sixth century: Seaford, *Reciprocity*, pp. 245-6 and 'Dionysia', in *OCD*[3], p. 476.

43. For an account of the rituals and processions which preceded tragic performance at the Dionysia, see E. Csapo and W.J. Slater, *The Context of Ancient Drama* (Ann Arbor: University of Michigan Press, 1995), p. 105, and for a detailed reconstruction, C. Sourvinou-Inwood, *Tragedy and Athenian Religion*, pp. 67-140.

44. Aristotle (*Poetics*, 1449a10) derives tragedy from Dionysus' dithyramb and comedy from the phallic songs sung in his honour.

45. Detienne, *Dionysos at Large*, pp. 27-41; Burkert, *Greek Religion*, p. 163; W.K.C. Guthrie, *The Greeks and Their Gods* (Boston, MA: Beacon, 1955), p. 177. Henrichs, 'Greek and Roman Glimpses', pp. 3-4 denies the distinction.

46. The eponymous king of Icarion in north-east Attica, an area with particularly strong theatrical interests in the fifth century: Pickard Cambridge, *Dramatic Festivals*, pp. 48-9.

47. Details of this story come variously from Hyginus *Astronomy* 2.4; Eratosthenes, *Catasterismata* 8; Pausanias 1.2.5-6; an ancient commentator (scholiast) on Aristophanes *Acharnians* 243; Philochorus *FGrH* 328 F5.

48. Segal, *Dionysiac Poetics*, p. 16.

49. Isocrates *Panathenaicus* 123. Thebes had long been an implacable enemy of its neighbour Athens. On Thebes in Athenian tragedy, see F. Zeitlin, 'Thebes: Theatre of Self and Society in Athenian

Drama', in J. Winkler and F. Zeitlin (editors) *Nothing to do with Dionysos?: Athenian drama in its Social Context* (Princeton, NJ: Princeton University Press, 1990), pp. 130-67; Seaford, *Commentary*, p. 49.

50. Versnel, *Ter Unus*, pp. 151-5.

51. Sometimes he rescues his mother Semele (Iophon *TGrF* 22 F 3; Diodorus Siculus 4.25.4, Apollodorus 3.5.3) while in Aristophanes' *Frogs*, he goes there to retrieve a poet.

52. Burkert, *Ancient Mystery Cults* p. 22, *Greek Religion*, p. 293; see also F. Graf, 'Dionysian And Orphic Eschatology: New Texts and Old Questions', pp. 239-58 in *Masks*.

53. Burkert, *Greek Religion*, pp. 276-304, and in *Ancient Mystery Cults*. For a different view, Henrichs, *OCD*, p. 479. See Seaford, *Commentary*, pp. 39-44, who has gone furthest in interpreting the *Bacchae* through the lens of mystery cult.

54. Cf. n. 29 above. The Dionysiac festival of the Oschophoria at Athens featured a race performed by youths dressed in women's clothes and Euripides emphasises the ambiguous genders of Dionysus himself and of his 'warlike' female worshippers: 'Transvestite Dionysos', J.N. Bremmer in M. Padilla, *Rites of Passage in Ancient Greece: Literature, Religion, Society* (Lewisburg and London: Bucknell University Press: 1999), pp. 183-200.

55. Cf. Otto, *Dionysus*, p. 138; Burkert, *Ancient Mystery Cults*, pp. 104-5.

56. On the nature of Dionysus' identification with his worshippers, see Henrichs, 'He Has a God', in *Masks*, pp. 20-1, and in 'Male Intruders among the Maenads: the So-called Male Celebrant', in H. Evjen (editor), *Mnemai: Classical Studies in Memory of Karl K. Hulley* (Chico, CA: Scholars Press, 1984), pp. 69-91.

57. The subject and even existence of a developed and systematic 'Orphic' philosophy or theology is, however, rather controversial, since it depends on heterogeneous sources and much scholarly ingenuity. For a highly sceptical approach, see R. Edmonds, 'Tearing Apart the Zagreus Myth: A Few Disparaging Remarks on Orphism and Original Sin', *Classical Antiquity* 18 (1999), pp. 35-73.

58. Cf. Herodotus 2.81; Euripides *Hippolytus* 953-4; Burkert, *Greek Religion*, pp. 295-301. A vase of *c.* 440-30 combines a picture of Dionysus, a satyr and a Maenad with the death of Orpheus at the hands of Maenads: C. Houser, *Dionysos and his Circle: Ancient through Modern* (Cambridge, MA: Fogg Art Museum, 1979), pp. 12-24 (12).

59. Plato *Cratylus* 400c, *Laws* 701c: Burkert, *Greek Religion*, p. 297 offers a full list of sources. In Egypt, Dionysus is identified with Osiris, who also undergoes dismemberment, while J. Kott, *The Eating of the Gods* (New York: Random House, 1970), pp. 186-230, offers an interpretation of the story which outlines its parallels with elements in the story of Christ.

60. Burkert *Greek Religion*, p. 298; Otto, *Dionysus*, p. 103; Seaford *Reciprocity*, pp. 284-5. Pausanias 8.37.3 ascribes the first account of Dionysus' murder by the Titans to the sixth-century writer Onomacritus.

61. Burkert, *Ancient Mystery Cults*, p. 78; Seaford *Reciprocity*, pp. 283-4.

62. J. Winkler and F. Zeitlin (editors), *Nothing to do with Dionysos?: Athenian Drama in its Social Context* (Princeton, NJ: Princeton University Press, 1990). p. 1; Easterling, 'A Show for Dionysus', p. 45.

63. A detailed summary is found in Oranje, *Euripides' Bacchae*, pp. 124-30; cf. Dodds, *Commentary*, xxviii-xxxiii.

64. Fragments can be found in Hugh Lloyd-Jones' appendix to *Aeschylus*, translated by H.W. Smyth (Cambridge, MA: Harvard University Press, 1963), vol. 2.

65. For a detailed account of evidence for the plays in Aeschylus' Lycurgus story, see M. West, 'Tragica VII', *Bulletin of the Institute of Classical Studies* 39 (1983), pp. 63-82.

66. J. March, 'Euripides' Bakchai: A Reconstruction in the Light of Vase Painting', *Bulletin of the Institute of Classical Studies* 36 (1989), pp. 33-65. This is especially plausible in the light of *Bacchae* 47-52, 228, 231-2, 302-4, which prophesy a forthcoming battle between Dionysus and Pentheus: it is typical of Euripides to hint at one dramatic outcome and surprise his audience with another.

67. ARV[2] 16,14: C. Houser, *Dionysos and his Circle: Ancient through Modern* (Cambridge, MA: Fogg Art Museum, 1979), p. 102.

3. Analysis of the *Bacchae*

1. D. Wiles, *Tragedy in Athens: Performance Space and Theatrical Meaning* (Cambridge: Cambridge University Press, 1997), pp. 171-4, suggests that Semele's tomb was represented by an altar and a vine-covered pillar, and that the Chorus, during their *parodos*, would have brought in a statue of the god (84-8) and set it near Semele's memorial as a constant reminder of the god's presence.

2. Seaford, *Commentary*, pp. 155-7 is a superb introduction to the *parodos*.

3. Terms important for Bacchic worship are explained in the Glossary, pp. 171-2 below.

4. Winnington Ingram, *Euripides and Dionysus*, pp. 106-7.

5. Here assimilated to the Cretan Curetes just as Cretan Rhea (mother of Zeus who, in his Cretan incarnation, resembles Dionysus in being a youthful god who dies) is assimilated to the Anatolian mother-goddess. Dionysus' rites are easily assimilated to other Eastern ecstatic rites: Leinieks, *City of Dionysos*, pp. 304-8.

6. The word *sophia* (and cognates) is important in the play. It can denote anything from mere cleverness to a true wisdom with a moral dimension: the slippage between those two senses is used by Euripides to explore the complexity of Dionysus-cult and the implications of endorsing it: see also Chapter 4.

7. The reason for Actaeon's punishment is unclear. In the oldest version of the story (Stesichorus fr. 68 from Hesiod), he competed with Zeus for Semele, but once the tradition fixed Semele as his aunt, other stories arose such as that he courted Artemis or (as apparently here) boasted that he was a superior hunter to her. The best-known story about Actaeon – that he saw Artemis naked – is not attested until Callimachus (Hymn 5) in the third century BCE.

8. It is generally assumed that this is a reference to the smiling mask worn by the god: on its significance, see p. 100 below.

9. *Bacchae* 513 implies that the Chorus beat their drums at this point: the growing tension between Pentheus and Dionysus would be heightened by their drumming to express support for their leader and hostility to their enemy.

10. Pentheus' father was Echion, the offspring of the dragon's teeth which Cadmus sowed in the ground (265, 507, 995-6, 1025, 1155, 1274).

11. At 1065, Euripides conveys the slow descent of the treetop by the threefold repetition, unique in tragedy, of *'katêgen, êgen, êgen'* (translatable as 'pulled it down, down, down').

12. The same lines occur at the end of four other Euripidean plays: on their function, see D. Roberts, 'Parting Words: Final Lines in Sophocles and Euripides', *Classical Quarterly* 37 (1987), pp. 51-64.

13. The fullest attempt to recreate the lost parts of the *Bacchae* from the *Christus Patiens* is made by A. Kirkhoff, 'Ein Supplement zu Euripides *Bacchae*', *Philologus* 8 (1853), pp. 78-94; cf. Dodds, *Commentary*, pp. 243-5.

14. C. Willink, 'Some Problems in the *Bacchae*', *Classical Quarterly* (1966), pp. 16, 27-50, 220-42 (44-4); C. Segal, 'Lament and Recognition'. Seaford, *Commentary*, p. 252 argues that the lacuna included a reference to the establishment of Dionysus' cult at Thebes: against this, see R. Friedrich, 'Dionysus among the Dons: The New Ritualism in Richard Seaford's Commentary on the *Bacchae*', *Arion* 7 (2000), pp. 115-52 (139-41).

4. Under the Influence

1. Chapter 2, above, pp. 23, 31.

2. Both the third and fourth stasima contain repeated refrains. These are common in Aeschylus but not in later tragedy.

3. 'Dionysus' and 'Euripides' Dionysus' are not identical, since the god of tragedy is more colourful than the god of cult (cf. above, pp. 26-9). However, the question is one of degree: certain elements – especially those of ambiguity and detachment – are common to Dionysus in both cult and drama, even if they are especially emphasised in the latter.

4. Hints at revelation: *Bacchae* 502, cf. 518 and 923. At 498, the stranger prophesies that the god will save him; at 614, he states that he has saved himself. Distancing: 466, 494, 496, 518, 629-30, 825, 849, 975-6.

5. In earlier art Dionysus is bearded, but during the fifth century, artists begin to portray him as a beardless youth. Already in Aeschylus' *Edoni* fr. 60-2 he is mocked for effeminacy and in Aristophanes *Frogs* 46 he is mocked for his female dress. This change is probably influenced by Greek stereotypes of Easterners: a Dionysus associated with the East will be feminised.

6. Lost in translation is the similarity in sound between 'Dionysus' and 'Dios', the possessive form of 'Zeus', in Greek, which underlines the truth of the relationship between them: 'Dionysus (son) of Dios'.

7. *Bacchae* 89-100, cf. 292-5. Dionysus is not the only god whose birth avoids a mother's womb: Athena famously came from Zeus' head. A world in which men do not need women for the continuation of their line is a common fantasy in tragedy – Euripides *Medea* 573-5, *Hippolytus* 618-24 – but whereas Athena is reliably male-identified (Aeschylus *Eumenides* 736-8), Dionysus is dangerously sympathetic to barbarians and females, even to the extent of lending them his powers (*Bacchae* 1079-81, 1088-9, 1127-8).

8. Another loss in translation: *paedagogus* derives from the Greek words for 'child' and 'to lead'. At 211, in another confusion of categories, Cadmus offers to be an 'interpreter' (*prophêtês*) for Tiresias, tragedy's most famous *prophêtês*: Dodds, *Commentary*, p. 97.

9. Cf. Chapter 1, p. 12 above. Maenads play with the young of wild creatures and occasionally suckle them in art: Dodds, *Commentary*, p. 163.

10. One of his cult titles is 'Lysios' or 'Liberator': cf. p. 126 n. 13 above.

11. *Dei* is connected with the verb *deo* – I bind. On these verbs, see pp. 75-6.

12. Their enthusiastic references to northern Greece (410ff., 571) are probably small compliments to Euripides' host Archelaus of Macedon.

13. A detail that agrees with what we know of actual Dionysiac cult: Dionysiac bands were apparently even open to slaves.

14. The Greek text of *Bacchae* 1005-10 is disputed but its general outline is clear.

15. Cf. Winnington Ingram, *Euripides and Dionysus*, pp. 92-6, 115, 130.

16. Iron is closely connected with masculinity in the play and especially with Pentheus and his failed attempts at conquering Dionysus: 231, 736, 764, 1207. Segal, *Dionysiac Poetics*, pp. 61-7, argues that Dionysus presides over an alarming movement away from technological progress in this passage.

17. A detail attested on vases: ARV^2 833.14, contemporary with the *Bacchae*, shows a Maenad carrying a child by one leg over her shoulder.

18. I write as the battle about same-sex marriage rages in the United States.

19. Herodotus 3.80 lists the commonest stereotypes of the tyrant. Creon in Sophocles' *Antigone* is a good example of the tragic tyrant, and is often compared with Pentheus: Dodds, *Commentary*, p. 97.

20. Compare the reactions of Oedipus and Creon to Tiresias, in Sophocles *Oedipus the King* 216-428 and *Antigone* 1055.

21. A common Euripidean technique: compare his treatment of Jason and Hippolytus at the ends of *Medea* and *Hippolytus* respectively.

22. The word for peace (*hêsuchos*, 622, 636) is the same as that used by the Chorus to describe Dionysiac peace.

23. He also describes the god as one who 'keeps company' with young girls (237): this verb (*suggignetai*) has sexual connotations in Greek.

24. One might recall the initial outrage at long-haired men in the 1960s, while a recent well-known piece of research argues that men who react most negatively to gay men tend themselves to find homosexual images attractive: H.E. Adams and others, 'Is Homophobia Associated With Homosexual Arousal?', *Journal of Abnormal Psychology* 105 (1996), pp. 440-5.

25. *Bacchae* 485-7; cf. Euripides *Ion* 550-5, Livy, *History of Rome* 39.9-10. Versnel, *Ter Unus*, pp. 100-20; J. March, 'Euripides' Bakchai: A Reconstruction in the Light of Vase Painting', *Bulletin of the Institute of Classical Studies* 36 (1989), pp. 33-65.

26. See, for example, Euripides' *Medea* or Aristophanes' *Thesmophoriaszousae*.

27. The loom symbolises the lives of women before they have been liberated by Dionysus: 118-9, 514. At 1252, Agave prays that her son be a great hunter, like his mother: Greek men commonly wish for prowess similar to, or greater than, their own for their sons (cf. Homer *Iliad* 6.476-81). Agave has temporarily assumed a male role under Dionysus (cf. *Bacchae* 764): such role reversal will prove destructive and her heroic power illusory.

28. As Winnington Ingram, *Euripides and Dionysus*, pp. 20-1.

29. Infliction of humiliation and violence (*hybris*) is typical of the tyrant: Herodotus 3.80.3.

30. The change in dress is not strictly necessary, but indicates the god's control over him: Dodds, *Commentary*, p. 181. Although the detail recalls Greek ritual practices (p. 127 n. 29), one need not assume that a ritual is literally being performed here. Dionysus insists on women's clothing quite simply because it will humiliate Pentheus.

31. Though particularly striking here, they are prevalent throughout the play: C. Segal, 'Etymologies and Double Meanings in Euripides' *Bacchae*', *Glotta* 60 (1982), pp. 81-93.

32. A willing victim was essential for the efficacy of a sacrifice and Pentheus goes willingly to Cithaeron: B. Seidensticker, 'Sacrificial Ritual in the *Bacchae*', in *Arktouros, Hellenic Studies Presented to Bernard M.W. Knox* (Berlin: de Gruyter, 1979), pp. 181-90.

33. Or, 'make me dis-solute' (cf. Segal, *Dionysiac Poetics*, p. 202), since the Greek verb is *truphan*, which derives from *thrupto* 'break in little pieces'.

34. The silence before the final slaughter resembles the sacrificial pattern of silence, then prayer, before a ritual killing.

35. The creature is a lion (1142, 1174, 1196, 1215, 1278) and occasionally a bull (1185). Both animals have Dionysiac associations: a lion is associated with the hunt while the bull Pentheus echoes the bull Dionysus: Seaford, *Commentary*, p. 244. Both animals are violent, yet their youth is also emphasised through the way Agave strokes the head (1185f.): Pentheus and Dionysus themselves share in this mixture of the violent and the tender.

36. The practice is normal for animal skulls but only barbarians or evildoers nail up human skulls: Dodds, *Commentary*, p. 227.

37. On Cadmus' 'psychoanalysis' of Agave, see G. Devereux, 'The Psychotherapy Scene in Euripides' *Bacchae*', *Journal of Hellenic Studies* 90 (1970), pp. 35-48.

38. Dodds, *Commentary*, pp. 233-4; Seaford, *Commentary*, pp. 252-5.

39. For discussion of the question, see Oranje, *Euripides' Bacchae*, pp. 151-65.

40. Winnington Ingram, *Euripides and Dionysus*, pp. 94-7.

41. See Seaford, *Commentary*, pp. 114-5, 218-9. For a discussion of the problem see also M. Cropp, 'TI TO SOPHON?', *Bulletin of the Institute of Classical Studies* 28 (1981), pp. 39-42 and Leinieks, *City of Dionysos*, pp. 370-2.

42. P. Roth, 'Teiresias as Mantis and Intellectual in Euripides' *Bacchae*', *Transactions of the American Philological Society* 114 (1984), pp. 59-69; cf. Ch. 5 n. 20 below.

43. See B. Seidensticker, 'Comic Elements in Euripides' Bacchae', *American Journal of Philology* 99 (1978), pp. 303-20: Seaford, *Commentary*, p. 167 doubts that the scene is comic. S. Goldhill, 'Doubling and Recognition in the *Bacchae*', *Metis* 3 (1988), pp. 137-55

(148) suggests that this unusual Tiresias demonstrates the power of Dionysus to transform those with whom he has contact.

44. Wordplay on *mantis* (prophet) and *mania* (madness) is not confined to 299: cf. Plato *Phaedrus* 244e.

45. Prodicus (84 B5 Diels Kranz) considered 'dry' and 'wet' as essential elements and identified Demeter and Dionysus with their most valuable forms: Dodds, *Commentary*, pp. 104-5.

46. In this interpretation, intellectual logic is simply inadequate for talking about Dionysus: those more hostile to him (as Winnington Ingram, *Euripides and Dionysus*, pp. 111-12) condemn the cult for anti-intellectualism on the same evidence.

47. But this may be too optimistic a view of Dionysus' actions as just and logical: Grube, *Drama of Euripides*, p. 419; Winnington Ingram, *Euripides and Dionysus*, p. 142.

48. It is true that Dionysus prophesies that even Cadmus will find rest eventually in the Land of the Blessed Ones (1339), but this is not the main focus of his speech and Cadmus himself entirely ignores this part of the prophecy (1360-2).

49. Thus Dionysus would have left the stage after 1351. Assigning this line to Cadmus also equalises the number of lines spoken by father and daughter: C. Willink, 'Some Problems in the *Bacchae*', *Classical Quarterly* 16 (1966), pp. 27-50, 220-42 (242). Seaford accepts the alteration while Dodds retains the transmitted text.

50. A woman's costume which can also connote a shroud: Aeschylus *Choephoroi* 998-1000.

51. Hunters are on the cusp of the civilised and wild worlds and walk a narrow tightrope between killing and being killed. Even the Chorus exemplify this ambiguity in describing themselves as fawns (865ff.) while wearing the skins of the fawns that they have killed: Winnington Ingram, *Euripides and Dionysus*, pp. 35, 106-7; Segal, *Dionysiac Poetics*, p. 35. Hunting offers a rich store of images to describe the shifting balance of power between Pentheus and Dionysus as hunter and hunted.

52. Metatheatre is the technical term for drama that emphasises its own theatrical elements: see pp. 100-2.

53. Cf. V. Castellani, 'That Troubled House of Pentheus in Euripides' *Bacchae*', *Transactions of the American Philological Association* 106 (1976), pp. 61-83.

54. At 1277, Agave asks whose *prosôpon* she holds. The word can mean a theatrical mask as well as a face or head: C. Segal, 'Etymologies and Double Meanings in Euripides' *Bacchae*', *Glotta* 60 (1982), pp. 81-93 (92).

55. See also p. 101. Dionysus' smile may be traditional: when captured by pirates in the Homeric hymn to Dionysus, he smiles (7.14), as he does on vase paintings such as ABV 275.8.

56. Compare especially Aristophanes *Thesmophoriazousae* 214-70; Foley, 'Masque', pp. 344, 356-7.

57. Some of these will be more plausible for an ancient audience, some – particularly those with a greater symbolic content – for a modern audience. This chapter has deliberately focussed on the significance of the *Bacchae* for its ancient audience, but it is difficult to ignore completely the play's deep contemporary resonance.

58. M. McDonald, 'L'extase de Penthée; ivresse et réprésentation dans les Bacchantes d'Euripide', *Pallas* 38 (1992), pp. 227-37 (230).

59. W. Sale, *Existentialism and Euripides: Sickness, Tragedy and Divinity in the Medea, the Hippolytus and the Bacchae* (Berwick: Aureal, 1977), pp. 97-9. Many modern productions of the play hint at something similar: see p. 111.

5. Dionysus Dismembered: Critical Trends and the *Bacchae*

1. Silk and Stern, *Nietzsche on Tragedy*, p. 5; A. Michelini, *Euripides and the Tragic Tradition* (Wisconsin: Wisconsin University Press, 1987), pp. 3-51.

2. Cf. A. Michelini, *Euripides and the Tragic Tradition* (Wisconsin: Wisconsin University Press, 1987), pp. 277-8, 315-16.

3. Many critics discuss the multiplicity of interpretations which the *Bacchae* has generated: Goldhill, 'Modern Critical Approaches', is particularly helpful. The best antidote to one-sided interpretations of Dionysus is to compare the view of three or more modern scholars: Henrichs, 'Greek and Roman Glimpses', p. 1, n. 1. I have attempted to do so in this chapter, although I make no claims to completeness. I also concentrate on the currents of interpretation that dominate English language criticism, but for a more broadly-based selection of European scholarly opinion, see H. Merklin, *Gott und Mensch im 'Hippolytos' und den 'Bakchen' des Euripides* (Freiburg, 1964), pp. 30-9 and Oranje, *Euripides' Bacchae*, pp. 7-18. P. McGinty, *Interpretation and Dionysus: Method in the Study of a God* (The Hague: Mouton, 1978) explores the theories of four earlier seminal scholars – Rohde, Harrison, Nilsson and Otto.

4. A.W. Verrall, *Euripides, the Rationalist: A Study in the History of Arts and Religion* (Cambridge: Cambridge University Press, 1895); Dodds, 'Euripides the Irrationalist', in E.R. Dodds, *The Ancient Concept of Progress and other Essays in Greek Literature and Belief* (Oxford: Clarendon Press, 1973), pp. 78-91.

5. Nietzsche, *The Birth of Tragedy* (Basel, 1871). For a useful summary of this book, see Silk and Stern, *Nietzsche on Tragedy*, pp. 62-89; also J.I. Porter, *The Invention of Dionysus: An Essay on The Birth of Tragedy* (Stanford, CA: Stanford University Press, 2000). On Nietzsche and the *Bacchae*, see Henrichs, 'Loss of Self'.

6. Nietzsche's 'principle of individuation' is represented by Dionysus' opponent Apollo and embodies 'respect for the limits of the individual, *moderation* in the Hellenic sense'. Nietzsche, *Birth*, section 4.

7. Nietzsche, *Birth*, section 1.

8. Cf. Silk and Stern, *Nietzsche on Tragedy*, p. 74. E. Faas in *Tragedy and After: Euripides, Shakespeare, Goethe* (Kingston and Montreal: McGill-Queen's University Press, 1984), p. 68ff. considers the *Bacchae* not tragic but 'post-tragic': tragedy should offer explanation for suffering, but the suffering inflicted on Pentheus and Agave seems neither meaningful nor ennobling.

9. Silk and Stern, *Nietzsche on Tragedy*, pp. 96ff., 253, 258.

10. E. Rohde, *Psyche*, originally published in 1894 and translated by W.B. Hillis (London: K. Paul, Trench, Trubner, 1925).

11. Silk and Stern, *Nietzsche on Tragedy*, pp. 163-4; Henrichs, 'He Has a God', p. 23.

12. Dodds, *Commentary*; Segal, *Dionysiac Poetics*; J.P. Vernant, 'The Masked Dionysus', in *Myth and Tragedy in Ancient Greece* (New York: Zone, 1988), pp. 381-412.

13. Cf. Easterling, 'A Show for Dionysus'. The cover of Paul Wooodruff's translation of the *Bacchae* depicts the young Elvis Presley before Dionysiac excess took its toll. J.Z. Smith, 'The Devil in Mr. Jones', in *Imagining Religion from Babylon to Jonestown* (Chicago: University of Chicago Press, 1982), pp. 102-20, invokes Dionysus in his account of Jim Jones, the charismatic cult leader who led his people to mass suicide in Guyana.

14. Versnel, *Ter Unus*, p. 96. Winnington Ingram, *Euripides and Dionysus*, p. 4; Norwood, *The Riddle of the Bacchae* (Manchester: Manchester University Press, 1908), p. 81 offers a list of believers and sceptics.

15. A.J. Festugière, 'Euripide dans Les Bacchantes', *Eranos* 55 (1957), pp. 127-44 (138-9); M. Orban 'Les Bacchantes: Euripide fidèle a lui-meme', *Les Etudes Classiques* 52 (1984) pp. 217-32. Even Winnington Ingram, *Euripides and Dionysus*, p. 6, and Dodds, *Commentary*, p. xlvii, are a little seduced.

16. Cf. Dodds' thumbnail sketch of the theory in European criticism, *Commentary*, pp. xl-xli.

17. A.W. Verrall, *The Bacchae of Euripides and Other Essays* (Cambridge, 1910), esp. pp. 108, 134-5. See, however, Dodds, *Commentary*, pp. xlviii-xlix.

18. G. Norwood, *The Riddle of the Bacchae* (Manchester: Manchester University Press 1908), pp. 73, 84; cf. also 39-49. His *Essays on Euripidean Drama* (Berkeley, CA: University of California Press, 1954) modifies this extreme position: he came to believe in the stranger's divinity, though not the literal destruction of the palace.

19. Dodds, *Commentary*, p. xl: 'Why did Euripides, tireless innovator and experimenter as he had always been, leave as his final legacy to his fellow-countrymen this topical yet deeply old-fashioned miracle play ... Had he some lesson which he wished to teach them?' It is possible to place excessive significance on the chronological accident that the *Bacchae* is Euripides' latest play, and recent critics, such as Seaford, *Commentary*, pp. 50-1, question the validity of questions like these.

20. These intellectuals are often known as the Sophists. They espoused relativism and scepticism regarding traditional values, and as such attracted suspicion from more traditionally-minded Greeks. On their unpopularity at Athens, see Oranje, *Euripides' Bacchae*, pp. 46-7: cf. also Ch. 4 nn. 42, 45 above.

21. Anti-Tiresias: Grube, *Drama of Euripides*, p. 404; Winnington Ingram, *Euripides and Dionysus*, pp. 42-57; cf. Dodds, *Commentary*, p. 91. More favourably, Conacher, *Euripidean Drama*, p. 62.

22. G. Norwood, *The Riddle of the Bacchae* (Manchester: Manchester University Press, 1908), p. 66; Dodds, *Commentary*, p. xliii, n. 1 cites other pro-Pentheus critics; see also Oranje, *Euripides' Bacchae*, pp. 8-9.

23. Oranje, *Euripides' Bacchae*, p. 64; E.M. Blaiklock, *The Male Characters of Euripides* (Wellington: New Zealand University Press, 1952), pp. 214-16; J. March, 'Euripides' Bakchai: A Reconstruction in the Light of Vase Painting', *Bulletin of the Institute of Classical Studies* 36 (1989) pp. 33-65 (44-6); Winnington Ingram, *Euripides and Dionysus,* pp. 44-7.

24. Dodds, *Commentary*, p. xxiv; Versnel, *Ter Unus*, pp. 103-30, 160-2. It is typical of advocates of state control to be suspicious of private mystery cults: Burkert, *Ancient Mystery Cults*, p. 11.

25. Dodds, *Commentary*, p. xliii; L. Greenwood, *Aspects of Euripidean Tragedy* (New York: Russell and Russell, 1952), p. 54; cf. Winnington Ingram, *Euripides and Dionysus*, pp. 58, 77.

26. J. Sandys, *Euripides' Bacchae* (Cambridge: Cambridge University Press, 1900), p. lxii; Oranje, *Euripides' Bacchae*, p. 42.

27. Cf. pp. 58-9 above; Segal, *Dionysiac Poetics*, p. 56; *contra* G. Norwood, *The Riddle of the Bacchae* (Manchester: Manchester University Press 1908), pp. 58-9.

28. Oranje, *Euripides' Bacchae*, pp. 60-70; J. Gregory, 'Some Aspects of Seeing in Euripides' Bacchae', *Greece and Rome* 32 (1985), pp. 23-31 (24); J. March, 'Euripides' Bakchai: A Reconstruction in the Light of Vase Painting', *Bulletin of the Institute of Classical Studies* 36 (1989) pp. 33-65 (49).

29. Foley, 'Masque', p. 345; Grube, *Drama of Euripides*, p. 401; *contra* Winnington Ingram, *Euripides and Dionysus* pp. 20-1.

30. Conacher, *Euripidean Drama*, pp. 50-2 , 58-9. A. Burnett,

'Pentheus and Dionysus: Host and Guest', *Classical Philology* 65 (1970), pp. 15-29.

31. Conacher, *Euripidean Drama*, p. 72; implied also by Dodds, 'Euripides the Irrationalist', in E.R. Dodds, *The Ancient Concept of Progress and other Essays in Greek Literature and Belief* (Oxford: Clarendon Press, 1973), pp. 102-3, but qualified by W. Sale, *Existentialism and Euripides: Sickness, Tragedy and Divinity in the Medea, the Hippolytus and the Bacchae* (Berwick: Aureal, 1977), p. 82f. and by others who interpret Dionysus more symbolically.

32. Winnington Ingram, *Euripides and Dionysus*, pp. 5, 66-9, 95, 113, 116, 178. See also Easterling, 'A Show for Dionysus', p. 36.

33. The words of Dodds, *Commentary*, p. xlvi, which refer to Euripides' portrayal of his typical heroes, supply a warning to Euripidean critics as well: 'his favourite method is to take a one-sided view, a noble half-truth, to exhibit its nobility, and then exhibit the disaster to which it leads its blind adherents – because it is after all only part of the truth.'

34. Segal, *Dionysiac Poetics*, pp. 13-15, 55-6; M. McDonald, 'L'extase de Penthée; ivresse et réprésentation dans les Bacchantes d'Euripide', *Pallas* 38 (1992), pp. 227-37 (229-30).

35. Segal, *Dionysiac Poetics*, p. 20. For a different interpretation which maintains the idea of ambiguity but argues that Pentheus and Dionysus are both right and both wrong, see Versnel, *Ter Unus*, pp. 173-6.

36. A. Michelini, *Euripides and the Tragic Tradition* (Wisconsin: Wisconsin University Press, 1987), p. 107.

37. Oranje, *Euripides' Bacchae*, pp. 11-14 summarises critical opinion on both sides of the argument.

38. L. Greenwood, *Aspects of Euripidean Tragedy* (New York: Russell and Russell, 1952), pp. 8, 29; A.W. Verrall, *The Bacchae of Euripides and Other Essays* (Cambridge: Cambridge University Press, 1910), p. 17; *contra* Winnington Ingram, *Euripides and Dionysus*, pp. 7-8.

39. Winnington Ingram, *Euripides and Dionysus*, p. 14; Grube, *Drama of Euripides*, p. 42.

40. Sourvinou-Inwood, *Tragedy and Athenian Religion*, esp. pp. 19, 31-47, 153, 177-8, 294-300, 330-1, 410-16.

41. For example, W. Sale, *Existentialism and Euripides: Sickness, Tragedy and Divinity in the Medea, the Hippolytus and the Bacchae* (Berwick: Aureal, 1977), p. 82; M. McDonald, 'L'extase de Penthée; ivresse et réprésentation dans les Bacchantes d'Euripide', *Pallas* 38 (1992), pp. 227-37; Segal, 'Pentheus on the Couch', p. 292 offers a psychoanalytically symbolic reading.

42. 'We tend to reduce the essential tension between the divine and human in Dionysus by scholarly allegorizing, by interpreting the god as a mere personification of powers located within the individual psyche or social environment.' Henrichs, 'He Has a God', p. 22.

43. L. Greenwood, *Aspects of Euripidean Tragedy* (New York: Russell and Russell, 1952), pp. 35-8.

44. Goldhill, *Reading Greek Tragedy* , pp. 259-61; Foley, 'Masque', p. 347.

45. Henrichs, 'He Has a God', pp. 30-1. Winnington Ingram, *Euripides and Dionysus*, p. 54 gives the changeability of Dionysus a darker cast as 'unstable emotion and violence'.

46. J.P. Vernant, 'Dionysus', in *The Encyclopedia of Religion* (New York: Macmillan, 1987), pp. 113-4; *Myth and Tragedy in Ancient Greece* (New York, 1988), pp. 398-400; cf. Henrichs. 'He Has a God', pp. 34-5.

47. Most fully expressed in his *Commentary*; see also 'Dionysiac Drama and the Dionysiac Mysteries', *Classical Quarterly* 31 (1981), pp. 252-75 and *Reciprocity,* pp. 233-405. Leinieks, *City of Dionysos*, also distrusts many current 'orthodoxies' of criticism of the *Bacchae* (especially the work of Charles Segal) but see the review by V. Wohl, *Classical Review* 49 (1999), pp. 10-11 for criticisms of Leinieks' approach.

48. This point is well made by Segal, 'Language of the Self', p. 305f., who argues that the mystic and the psychological are intertwined throughout the *Bacchae*. What is 'not to be spoken of' religiously is equally 'unspeakable in the problematical knowledge of the unconscious' which is 'at some level alienated from language'. Pentheus' trip to Cithaeron is both a mystic initiation through which Dionysus' divine power is revealed and a revelation of his inner conflicts and contradictions.

49. G. Murray, 'Excursus on the Ritual Forms in Greek Tragedy', in J. Harrison (editor), *Themis: A Study in the Social Origins of Greek Religion*, (Cambridge: Cambridge University Press, 1912) and in shortened form in G. Murray, *Euripides and His Age* (London: Oxford University Press, 1946), pp. 29-30; cf. Henrichs 'He Has a God', p. 27, n.34.

50. Segal, *Dionysiac Poetics*, p. 37; Goldhill, 'Modern Critical Approaches', p. 332.

51. Cf. Goff, *Citizen Bacchae*, pp. 290-1. For an excellent introduction to structuralist and psychological readings of tragedy, see also Segal, 'Pentheus on the Couch'.

52. S. des Bouvrie, 'Euripides *Bakkhai*', *Classica et Medievalia* 48 (1977), pp. 75-114 (80-3).

53. Cf. Goldhill, 'Modern Critical Approaches', pp. 334ff., Segal, 'Lament and Recognition'; *Dionysiac Poetics*, p. 58ff.; 'Pentheus on the Couch'; *Bacchae* as Metatragedy', p. 168.

54. Segal has traced some extremely complex patterns of reversal in the play which should be read in their entirety: 'Pentheus on the Couch', p. 285; 'Lament and Recognition, pp. 282-7; *Dionysiac Poetics*, pp. 164-8.

55. R. Seaford, 'Dionysus as Destroyer of the Household: Homer, Tragedy and the Polis', *Masks*, pp. 115-46 (134).

56. C. Segal, 'Euripides' *Bacchae*: Conflict and Mediation,' *Ramus* 6 (1977), pp. 103-20 (103-4).

57. Foley, 'Masque', p. 351, and for the connection of the *Bacchae* with actual ritual, see B. Seidensticker, 'Sacrificial Ritual in the *Bacchae*', in *Arktouros, Hellenic Studies Presented to Bernard M.W. Knox* (Berlin: de Gruyter, 1979) pp. 181-90.

58. *Homo Necans: the Anthropology of Ancient Greek Sacrificial Ritual and Myth*, translated by P. Bing (Berkeley, CA: University of California Press, 1983) p. 34, and, in general, see pp. 1-78 for the outline of a complex theory: I have greatly over-simplified it here and Burkert's work is fundamental to an important strain in criticism of the *Bacchae*. In *Totem and Taboo*, Freud also posited that social institutions are a product of violence between human beings: E. Faas, *Tragedy and After: Euripides, Shakespeare, Goethe* (Kingston and Montreal: McGill-Queen's University Press, 1984), p. 15.

59. René Girard, *Violence and the Sacred*, translated by Patrick Gregory (Baltimore: Johns Hopkins University Press, 1977), esp. pp. 119-42.

60. Dodds, *Commentary*, pp. 80-1, 209; B. Seidensticker, 'Sacrificial Ritual in the *Bacchae*', in *Arktouros, Hellenic Studies Presented to Bernard M.W. Knox* (Berlin: de Gruyter, 1979) pp. 181-90.

61. Girard, *Violence and the Sacred*, translated by Patrick Gregory (Baltimore: Johns Hopkins University Press, 1977), p. 132; cf. Henrichs, 'Loss of Self', p. 233.

62. Although Seaford, *Commentary*, p. 32 agrees that Girard's theory is problematic, he claims that the theme of unanimous violence against a scapegoat is so important in Greek religion and tragedy that it must have a core of truth: *contra* Henrichs, 'Loss of Self'; Goldhill, 'Modern Critical Approaches', p. 333; Bremmer 'Greek Maenadism Reconsidered'.

63. Seaford's views are most fully expressed in his *Commentary*, but see also 'Dionysiac Drama and the Dionysiac Mysteries', *Classical Quarterly* 31 (1981), pp. 252-75.

64. Cf. Segal, *Dionysiac Poetics*, pp. 169-70.

65. Seaford, *Commentary*, pp. 42-3: but for a highly sceptical discussion of his theories, see R. Friedrich, 'Dionysus among the Dons: the New Ritualism in Richard Seaford's Commentary on the *Bacchae*', *Arion* 7 (2000), pp. 115-52 (129-32).

66. As well as Friedrich, sceptics include Leinieks, *City of Dionysos*, pp. 123-51, who casts doubt on the existence of Dionysiac mystery cult at Athens; cf. also S. des Bouvrie, 'Euripides *Bakkhai*', *Classica et Medievalia* 48 (1977), pp. 75-114 (104). In 'Lament and Recognition', p. 290, Segal acknowledges the existence of initiatory elements in the play, but notes that they are used ironically: initiation leads neither to rebirth, nor to joy.

67. See J. Bremmer, 'Scapegoat Rituals in Ancient Greece', *Harvard Studies in Classical Philology* 87 (1983), pp. 299-320. For Seaford, *Commentary*, p. 226, Pentheus is 'assimilated' to the scapegoat, rather than a scapegoat in the technical sense: for forceful objections to the theory, see Leinieks, *City of Dionysos*, pp. 168-172; S. des Bouvrie, 'Euripides *Bakkhai* and Maenadism', *Classica et Medievalia* 48 (1997), pp. 75-114 (103).

68. Segal, *Dionysiac Poetics*, pp. 79, 382. I disagree with those who see Pentheus' death as a self-sacrifice for the city, such as J. March, 'Euripides' Bakchai: A Reconstruction in the Light of Vase Painting', *Bulletin of the Institute of Classical Studies* 36 (1989), pp. 33-65 (55-6). S. des Bouvrie, 'Euripides *Bakkhai*', *Classica et Medievalia* 48 (1977), pp. 75-114 (80-3), argues that tragedy concerns the disruption and later restoration of some fundamental societal institution – in the case of the *Bacchae*, Maenadic Dionysus-cult. However, her attempt to separate the unhappy dramatic ending from the symbolic nature of the drama, in which Pentheus' death affirms the women's cult, like all optimistic readings of the play, is difficult given Agave's comprehensive rejection of Dionysus.

69. Versnel, *Ter Unus*, esp. pp. 100-21.

70. So A. Podlecki, 'Individual and Group in Euripides' *Bacchae*', *Antiquité Classique* 43 (1974), pp. 143-65; B. Seidensticker, 'Pentheus', *Poetica* 6 (1972), pp. 35-63 notes that many of Pentheus' characteristics are found in Theodor Adorno's archetype of the Authoritarian Personality; cf. also Goldhill, 'Modern Critical Approaches', pp. 343-5.

71. J. Carrière, 'Sur le message des bacchantes', *Antiquité Classique* 35 (1966), pp. 118-39. J. de Romilly, 'Le thème du bonheur dans les *Bacchantes*', *Revue des Etudes Grecques* 76 (1963), pp. 361-80 offers a modified form of the theory, which links Euripidean pessimism and lack of faith in the gods with the mood at the end of the Peloponnesian war.

72. Seaford, *Commentary*, pp. 46-52 and 'Dionysus as Destroyer of the Household: Homer, Tragedy and the Polis', *Masks*, pp. 138. Leinieks' interpretation in *City of Dionysos* is similar in some respects and is almost unique among those of modern interpreters by denying – unconvincingly – that sexuality is in any way a theme of the play: e.g. pp. 6, 76 n. 2.

73. Segal, 'Lament and Recognition', pp. 289-91; *Dionysiac Poetics*, p. 382. The strongest collective voice in the play is not that of the democratic male city but that of the Chorus who are not Theban, male or even Greek: Goldhill, *Reading Greek Tragedy*, pp. 271-3.

74. As E.M. Blaiklock, *The Male Characters of Euripides: A Study in Realism* (Wellington: University of New Zealand Press, 1952).

75. E. Howald, *Die Griechische Tragödie* (Munich: Oldenbourg, 1930); W. Zürcher, *Die Darstellung des Menschen im Drama des Euripides* (Basel: Reinhardt, 1947).

76. J. Gould, 'Dramatic Character and "Human Intelligibility"', in Greek Tragedy', *Proceedings of the Cambridge Philological Society* 33 (1978), pp. 43-67.

77. C. Collard, *Euripides: Greece and Rome New Surveys in the Classics 14* (Oxford: Clarendon Press, 1981), p. 11; Seaford, *Commentary*, pp. 33-4. In general, see P. Easterling's very useful essay, 'Constructing Character in Greek Tragedy', in C. Pelling (editor), *Characterisation and Individuality in Greek Literature* (Oxford: Clarendon Press, 1990), pp. 81-99.

78. Goldhill, 'Modern Critical Approaches', pp. 340-2.

79. Dodds, *Commentary*, pp. xliii, 97-8.

80. W. Sale, 'The psychoanalysis of Pentheus in the Bacchae of Euripides', *Yale Classical Studies* 22 (1972), pp. 63-82, with a modified and more convincing treatment in *Existentialism and Euripides* (Berwick: Aureal, 1977), pp. 101-20; cf. M. Orban, 'Les *Bacchantes*: Euripide fidèle a lui-meme', *Les Etudes Classiques* 52 (1984), pp. 217-32 (226) and, for a particularly convincing argument, Segal, 'Pentheus on the Couch'. Against such approaches, see Oranje, *Euripides' Bacchae*, p. 14.

81. G. Devereux, 'The Psychotherapy Scene in Euripides' *Bacchae*', *Journal of Hellenic Studies* 90 (1970), pp. 35-48; cf. Segal, 'Language of the Self', p. 299, n. 11.

82. J. Gregory, 'Some Aspects of Seeing in Euripides' *Bacchae*', *Greece and Rome* 32 (1985), pp. 23-31 (24-9).

83. Material on the language and imagery of the play is abundant: see, for example, R. Dyer, 'Image and Symbol: The Link Between the Two Worlds of the "Bacchae"', *Journal of the Australasian Universities Language and Literature Association* 21 (1964), pp. 15-26; Winnington Ingram, *Euripides and Dionysus*, pp. 60, 106-7; S. Goldhill, 'Doubling and Recognition in the *Bacchae*', *Metis* 3 (1988), pp. 137-55 (esp. 141-4) and *Reading Greek Tragedy*, p. 259; Segal, *Dionysiac Poetics*, pp. 27-8, 58ff., 'Etymologies and Double Meanings in Euripides' *Bacchae*', *Glotta* 60 (1982), pp. 81-93; W. Scott, 'Two Suns Over Thebes: Imagery and Stage Effects in the *Bacchae*', *Transactions of the American Philological Association* 105 (1975) pp. 333-46; V. Castellani, 'That Troubled House of Pentheus in Euripides' *Bacchae*', *Transactions of the American Philological Association* 106 (1976), pp. 61-83.

84. Segal, 'Language of the Self'.

85. Dodds, *Commentary*, p. xvi: 'to resist Dionysus is to repress the elemental in one's one nature; the punishment is the sudden complete collapse of inward dykes when the elemental breaks through perforce and civilisation vanishes.' In spite of this, on pp. 153-4 he considers Winnington Ingram's suggestion that binding the bull is equivalent to constraining the animal Dionysus within himself 'over-subtle'.

86. Segal, 'Language of the Self', pp. 309-11; 'Pentheus on the Couch', pp. 282-3, 289-90; *Dionysiac Poetics*, p. 204.

87. Segal, *Dionysiac Poetics*, pp. 164-8.

88. As Leinieks, *City of Dionysos*, p. 6; cf. Oranje, *Euripides' Bacchae*, p. 14.

89. Foley, 'Masque', pp. 346-7; see also S. Goldhill, 'Doubling and Recognition in the *Bacchae*', *Metis* 3 (1988), pp. 137-55 (140); Segal, '*Bacchae* as Metatragedy'; *Dionysiac Poetics*, pp. 215-79. Not all critics accept such a concept as Euripidean: Seaford, *Commentary*, pp. 32-3 with references.

90. Segal, *Dionysiac Poetics*, pp. 223-4; on actors' understanding of the potential power of the mask, see Easterling, 'A Show for Dionysus', p. 51.

91. Foley, 'Masque', pp. 362, 346-7; Otto, *Dionysus*, pp. 86-91.

92. Foley, 'Masque', pp. 344-9.

93. Segal, '*Bacchae* as Metatragedy', p. 170.

94. Segal, '*Bacchae* as Metatragedy', pp. 157-9; Goldhill, *Reading Greek Tragedy*, pp. 278-9.

95. Seaford, *Commentary*, pp. 33, 214.

6. Singing! Orgies! Wine! Women! Song!

1. Taken from a poster advertising the play at Goucher College.

2. Lucas, *Euripides and His Influence*, p. 50; L. Edmunds, 'The Religiosity of Alexander', *Greek, Roman and Byzantine Studies* 12 (1971), pp. 363-91 (376-8).

3. C. Houser, 'Changing Views of Dionysos', in *Dionysos and His Circle* (Harvard: Fogg Museum, 1979) pp. 12-24.

4. A. Henrichs, 'Loss of Self', p. 212.

5. The programme for a 1964 production of the *Bacchae* at the Mermaid Theatre contains many advertisements from wine merchants and the slogan 'Unlucky Dionysus never had Guinysus'. (From the collection at the Oxford Archive of Performances of Greek and Roman Drama.)

6. Lucas, *Euripides and His Influence*, p. 57f.

7. For some apparent literary parallels between the *Bacchae* and the *Acts of the Apostles*, see R. Seaford, 'Thunder, Lightning and Earthquake in the Bacchae and the Acts of the Apostles', in A.B. Lloyd (editor), *What is a God? Studies in the Nature of Greek Divinity* (London: Duckworth, 1997), pp. 139-51.

8. For a brief history of the transmission of the *Bacchae*, see Dodds, *Commentary*, pp. li-lix.

9. P. Burian, 'Tragedy Adapted for Stage and Screens: the Renaissance to the Present', in Easterling, *Companion*, pp. 228-83 (229).

10. F. Zeitlin, 'Dionysus in 69', in *Dionysus Since 69*, pp. 49-76 (49-50), mentions the 1930s productions at Smith and Bryn Mawr Colleges in ancient costume.

11. For some particularly notable productions during this period, see J.M. Walton, *Living Greek Theatre: A Handbook of Classical Performance and Modern Production* (New York, Westport, CT and London: Greenwood Press, 1987), pp. 338-45.

12. Many thanks are due to the staff at the Archive for their help in providing these statistics. Their database is now on-line at http://www.apgrd.ox.ac.uk/database.

13. For accounts of some recent productions of the *Bacchae*, see H. Foley, 'Twentieth Century Performance and Adaptation of Euripides', *Illinois Classical Studies* 24-5 (1999-2001), pp. 1-13; K. Hartigan, *Greek Tragedy on the American Stage: Ancient Drama in the Commercial Theater, 1882-1994* (Westport, CT: Greenwood Press: 1995), pp. 82-89; M. Colakis, *The Classics and the American Theater of the 1960s and Early 1970s* (Lanham, MD: University Press of America, 1993), pp. 42-4; L. Hardwick, 'The Play's the Thing: Modern Staging of the *Bacchae*', *Dionysus* 15 (2001), pp. 24-9.

14. In *Dionysus Since 69*, pp. 2-3, Edith Hall cites a 1992 version of the play in Cameroon, in which an African businessman opposes a voodoo-influenced Rastafarian cult, a Chinese version at the Beijing Opera in 1996 and a Malaysian adaptation in 2001.

15. Quite typical is the Oberon Theatre Ensemble's apocalyptic *Bacchae Y2K* which is set during the Millennium extravaganza and makes greed and lust its central themes: see http://www.oobr.com/top/volSix/six/bacchae.html (1999). Similarly, Paul Schmidt describes his 1997 translation as 'a stunning take on what happens when you deny the irrational side of your mind ... it's about a man denying the feminine side of his nature': www.bostonphoenix.com/archive/theater/97/12/04/THE_BACCHAE.html.

16. R. Schechner, *Dionysus in 69* (New York: Farrar, Strauss and Giroux, 1970) contains all the variants of the script, actors' comments and photographs, but no page numbers. A film version by Brian de Palma also exists, but copies are hard to obtain. For an eyewitness account of the original production, see F. Zeitlin, 'Dionysus in 69', in *Dionysus Since 69*, pp. 49-76.

17. In one exercise, the women of the company made their own 'community' on the roofs near the performance space and gradually captured the men who went to look for them. Sadly, the activity was soon quashed by the police, alerted to possible gang activity.

18. M. Colakis, *The Classics and the American Theater of the 1960s and Early 1970s* (Lanham: University Press of America, 1993), p. 42. Schechner was influenced by Antonin Artaud, who is best known for his 'theatre of cruelty'. Artaud believed that theatre should liberate its audience from their repressions and that this could be achieved by removal of barriers between performers and audience and by the use of technical special effects to engender shock and awe in them.

19. The police chief condemned it as bad art but had not actually seen it (cf. *Bacchae* 216): Schechner, 'Radicalism, Sexuality and Performance', *Drama Review* 13 (1968), pp. 89-110 (94-6).

20. http://www.panix.com/~meejr/html/bacchae2.1.html.

21. L. Hardwick, 'The Play's the Thing: Modern Staging of the *Bacchae*', *Dionysus* 15 (2001), pp. 24-9 (27); K. Hartigan, *Greek Tragedy in the American Stage: Ancient Drama in the Commercial Theatre 1882-1994* (Westport, CT: Greenwood Press, 1995), p. 86.

22. W. Soyinka, *The Bacchae of Euripides: A Communion Rite* (New York: Norton, 1973), pp. vi-viii.

23. A. Nouryeh, 'Soyinka's Euripides: Postcolonial Resistance or Avant-garde Adaptation?', *Research in African Literatures*, 32 (2001), pp. 160-71 (161-2).

24. For Soyinka, the creative/destructive Yoruba god Ogun has some distinct similarities with Dionysus, although Ogun also contains elements of Apollo and Prometheus: E.D. Jones, *Wole Soyinka* (New York: Twayne Publishers, 1973), p. 15.

25. For example, Sheila Morgan's adaptation of the play begins as a group of figures recite the Lord's Prayer: gradually the rhythms of the words become wilder and lead to an orgiastic scene. This *Bacchae* dramatises an evolution of religious worship, from pagan rituals to Christian prayer, and in it Pentheus and Dionysus represent a contrast between the strictures of organized religion and spontaneous human spirituality: http://www.oobr.com/top/volSeven/seven/0910bacchae.html. Andrew Rissik's radio play, *Dionysus* (2003) assimilates Dionysus to Christ and Pentheus to Pontius Pilate.

26. To experience 'What suffering is. Feel the taste of blood instead of merely foreseeing it': Soyinka, p. 12. The idea that Dionysiac violence offers a special intensity through which the essence of life is seen more clearly recurs in Donna Tartt's *The Secret History*, in which a group of Classics students recreate a Bacchic *sparagmos* but accidentally kill an innocent farmer. One of the perpetrators, Henry, claims that the murder enabled him to get in touch with himself and 'live without thinking': D. Tartt, *The Secret History* (New York: Knopff, 1992), pp. 448-9.

27. R. Baker-White, 'The Politics of Ritual in Wole Soyinka's "The *Bacchae* of Euripides"', *Comparative Drama* 27 (1993), pp. 377-98 interprets this and other apparent anachronisms as 'Western popularist forms of contemporary ritual' (380) which depend on a group solidarity born of communal scapegoating.

28. The story is taken from Herodotus 6.129-30, in which Hippoclides loses his chance at a fine marriage by getting drunk and dancing upside down on the table.

29. Cf. H. Foley, 'Twentieth Century Performance and Adaptation of Euripides', *Illinois Classical Studies* 24-5 (1999-2001), pp. 1-13 (5-6).

30. A. Nouryeh, 'Soyinka's Euripides: Postcolonial Resistance or Avant-garde Adaptation?', *Research in African Literatures* 32 (2001), pp. 160-71 (167-70).

31. K. Hartigan, *Greek Tragedy in the American Stage: Ancient Drama in the Commercial Theatre 1882-1994* (Westport, CT: Greenwood Press, 1995), pp. 88-9.

32. For a more detailed account, see M. McDonald, *Ancient Sun, Modern Light: Greek Drama on the Modern Stage* (New York: Columbia University Press, 1992), pp. 59-73.

33. For further details of operas inspired by the *Bacchae*, see P. Burian, 'Tragedy Adapted for Stage and Screens: the Renaissance to the Present', in Easterling, *Companion*, pp. 228-83 (269) and P. Brown, 'Greek Tragedy in the Opera House and Concert Hall of the late Twentieth Century', in *Dionysus Since 69*, pp. 285-309 (286-291).

34. H. Partch, *Genesis of a Music: An Account of a Creative Work, its Roots and its Fulfillments*, 2nd edition (New York: Da Capo Press, 1979), cited by the programme notes of the 1987 recording of *Revelation in the Courthouse Park* by the American Music Theater Festival (Tomato Records, 1989).

35. Gender ambiguity is a staple theme in rock music: M. Jameson, 'The Asexuality of Dionysus', in *Masks*, pp. 44-64 (62). Soyinka explicitly portrays his slave leader as a rock star (above, p. 109). For an enjoyable comparison of the *Bacchae* with some elements of the *Rocky Horror Show*, see A. Aviram, 'Postmodern Gay Dionysus: Dr. Frank N. Furter', *Journal of Popular Culture* 26 (1992), pp. 183-92.

36. R. Bond, '(Re)inventing Euripides' *Bacchae*', in J. Barsby (editor), *Greek and Roman Drama: Translation and Performance* (Stuttgart and Weimar: J. B. Metzler, 2002), pp. 49-57 (55-6).

37. K. Hartigan, *Greek Tragedy in the American Stage: Ancient Drama in the Commercial Theatre 1882-1994* (Westport, CT: Greenwood Press, 1995), pp. 84, 88-9; T. Disch, *The Nation* 9/12/1987, p. 246. Reviews of the Guthrie Theatre production were otherwise lukewarm.

38. http://giardini.sm/projects/bakxai/trance/tranceframeeng.htm. The techniques of the 1998 production by the Performance Technology Research Laboratory at the Georgia Institute of Technology were similar in using special effects to transcend the standard theatrical experience: an advanced camera system sensed pre-programmed movements by the actors and triggered audio samplings according to their gestures. The audio clips could then be altered and played back at either random or scripted moments to disorient and surprise the audience: pictures are available at http://www.cc.gatech.edu/people/alumni/PhD/Colleen.Kehoe/bacchae/.

39. http://www.columbusalive.com/1997/19970819/theater.html.

40. J. Bowen, *The Disorderly Women* (London: Methuen, 1969): see also H. Foley, 'Bad Women: Gender Politics in Late 20th Century Performance and Revision of Greek Tragedy', in *Dionysus Since 69*, pp. 77-111.

41. Productions of the *Bacchae* in particular seem to swing between two poles of extreme modernism (e.g. *Dionysus in 69*) and a static, traditional approach (see the review by T. Disch, *The Nation* 9/12/1987, p. 247 of the Guthrie Theatre's 1987 production).

42. D. Wiles, 'The Use of Masks in Modern Performances of Greek Drama', in *Dionysus Since 69*, pp. 245-63.

43. See www.thiasos.co.uk. The company is directed by classical scholars.

44. Barbara Lewis, *The Stage*, 13th November 2003. Whether their strategy for performance really offers a more authentic rendition of tragedy is, of course, debatable.

45. For a discussion of the ways in which Pentheus and Dionysus can be crystallised into symbols of various fundamental conflicts, see Henrichs, 'Loss of Self', pp. 216-22.

46. A good example of the latter is Brian Friel's play *Wonderful Tennessee* (1993), the story of the uneasy relationships of three couples on the Donegal coast looking out at the sinister haunt of Dionysus, an island of mystic apparitions and human sacrifice. On Bacchic motifs in recent film, see M. McDonald, 'Moving Icons: Teaching Euripides in Film', in R. Mitchell-Boyask, *Approaches to Teaching the Dramas of Euripides* (New York: Modern Language Association of America, 2002), pp. 60-6 (63-5). P. McGinty, *Interpretation and Dionysus: Method in the Study of a God* (The Hague: Mouton, 1978), p. 3 discusses the Dionysian overtones of Thomas Mann's *Death in Venice*.

47. Oranje, *Euripides' Bacchae*, pp. 1-3.

48. *Rites* is found in V. Sullivan and J. Hatch (editors), *Plays By and About Women* (New York: Random House, 1973), pp. 349-77: see also H. Foley, 'Bad Women: Gender Politics in Late 20th Century Performance and Revision of Greek Tragedy', in *Dionysus Since 69*, pp. 77-111.

Texts, Commentaries and Translations

Gilbert Murray's *Oxford Classical Text* (Oxford: Clarendon Press, 1913), on which E.R. Dodds' still essential *Commentary* (Oxford: Oxford University Press, 1960) is based, is now superseded by James Diggle's 1994 *Oxford Classical Text* which is used (with some variants) by Richard Seaford in his *Commentary* (Warminster: Aris and Phillips, 1996). For those reading the play in Greek, Seaford's edition is good value, comprising a text with parallel translation, extensive endnotes and a substantial introduction: Seaford's thesis that Dionysiac mystery religion is central to the *Bacchae* is not, however, wholly accepted (cf. the review by S. Philippo, *Classical Review* 47 (1997), pp. 252-3), and it is prominent in this edition. A.S. Way's Loeb parallel text has now been replaced by the much superior Loeb of David Kovacs (Cambridge, MA: Harvard University Press, 2002).

The *Bacchae* has been abundantly served by translators, and for an overview of many currently in print (some of which I omit here), the survey by Charles Voinovich in his review of Paul Woodruff's translation in the *Bryn Mawr Classical Review* 2001-01-04 is essential: see also D. Roberts, 'Euripides in Translation', in R. Mitchell-Boyask (editor), *Approaches to Teaching the Dramas of Euripides* (New York: Modern Language Association of America, 2002), pp. 38-50. Because the *Bacchae* has been so popular over the last 30 years and because the conflict between Dionysus and Pentheus is frequently interpreted in the light of contemporary social conflicts, many translators render Euripides' Greek in colloquial English. One of the best is that of Stephen Esposito (Newburyport, MA: Focus, 1998) which includes a detailed introduction and ample help in notes which are useful for students with little experience in Greek or drama. This translation is now available in an anthology along with *Medea, Heracles* and *Hippolytus* (Newburyport, MA: Focus, 2002) with abbreviated but still abundant notes. Esposito translates in a straightforward and natural idiom and his translation would work both for Classics in translation courses and as a text for performance, since he also offers stage directions.

Another successful and helpful translation is that of Reginald Gibbons (New York: Oxford University Press, 2001). This series matches the translation of a poet with an introduction and notes to the play by a professional Classicist, and Gibbons' collaboration with Charles Segal has been fruitful. Unlike many of his contemporaries, Gibbons attempts to emulate the formal beauty of Euripides' language in his translation. In general, he is successful and his essay on translation is especially worth reading, while Segal's introduction and notes are based on his abundant contributions to Euripidean scholarship over the past decades. Unfortunately, his line numbers do not correspond to the Greek, so that the translation is harder to use than it might otherwise have been. As one would expect of a volume graced by a picture of Elvis Presley in army uniform, Paul Woodruff's translation (Indianapolis, IN: Hackett, 1998) uses a modern idiom: while he sometimes adds a little to Euripides, the translation is always crisp and clear. His useful 34-page introduction summarises some of the most influential interpretations of the play.

Other commonly available translations include the Penguin translation of Philip Vellacott, which is 50 years old and a little the worse for wear: no notes are provided, the translation is prosaic and adds material which is not in Euripides. William Arrowsmith's translation in David Grene & Richmond Lattimore, *Euripides*, vol. V (Chicago: Chicago University Press, 1959) has long reigned in American universities, and stands up well, but offers less help than recent editions geared to the needs of today's novices in Greek drama. The University of Pennsylvania Press has published a set of translations of Greek drama edited by David Slavitt and Palmer Bovie, but reviews have been mixed and the introduction to Daniel Epstein's 1998 translation contains some dubious statements: although the poetry of the choruses is lovely, such oddities as the encouragement to sing to the 'Evian God' (164) which would surely make many people think of water, rather than wine (Cana reversed!) do not make it the best choice.

G.S. Kirk's translation (Cambridge: Cambridge University Press, 1970) offers an introduction which, though influenced by Dodds and written before the reassessment of Bacchic cult by Henrichs and others, foreshadows their scepticism. Kirk's translation is faithful and literal and does not iron out Euripides' diction into a modern idiom. His notes are helpful and detailed, but try to be all things to all people: material useful for beginners sits alongside technical matters which would only be a concern to advanced readers. Notable emphasis is laid on metre, although the translation makes no attempt to reproduce the rhythms on which he lays emphasis. J. Michael Walton's *Bacchae* (London: Methuen, 1998) is a bare-bones translation less suitable for students who do not already know what a thyrsus is, but it is readable: its choruses are especially good, though they are perhaps not literal enough to use the translation with the Greek text. The translation of James Morwood (Oxford: Oxford University Press, 1999) contains a very useful introduction by

Edith Hall and handy endnotes, and is rendered in solid and accurate, if not especially poetic, prose.

Translations more suitable for reading or performance than as an aid to the Greek include that of Paul Roche (New York: Norton, 1974), who offers detailed instructions for a modern performance: his translation is readable, but not always close to the Greek. C.K. Williams' poetically memorable *Bacchae of Euripides* (New York: Noonday Press, 1990) contains an excellent introductory essay and bibliography by Martha Nussbaum, which is worth reading for its analysis of critical trends in the play. Derek Mahon's *Bacchae* (Oldcastle: Gallery Press, 1991), which he styles 'after Euripides', offers a colloquial translation in rhyming couplets, which works surprisingly well. Most recent is the translation of Colin Teevan (London: Oberon, 2002) with a brief introduction by Edith Hall. Like Sir Peter Hall's production for which it was commissioned (p. 117 above), his translation foregrounds the metatheatrical element in the play, and moves away from a literal rendition at a number of points in order to make emphatic some things which Euripides merely suggests or to provide necessary background information for the audience, but it is a powerful translation and worth reading.

Guide to Further Reading

Commentaries

Dodds, *Commentary*. E.R. Dodds, *Euripides: Bacchae* (Oxford: Oxford University Press, 1960). Unsurpassed in many ways, though its picture of Dionysiac religion should be viewed cautiously.

Seaford, *Commentary*. R. Seaford, *Euripides: Bacchae* (Warminster: Aris and Phillips, 1996). Emphasis (especially on mystery religion) very different from Dodds' and should be read alongside him.

Greek religion: general

Burkert, *Greek Religion*. W. Burkert, *Greek Religion*, translated by J. Raffan (Cambridge, MA: Harvard University Press, 1985). Learned, readable general guide to Greek religion.

Burkert, *Ancient Mystery Cults*. W. Burkert, *Ancient Mystery Cults* (Cambridge, MA: Harvard University Press, 1987). Reliable account of Dionysus and mystery religion.

Goff, *Citizen Bacchae*. B. Goff, *Citizen Bacchae: Women's Ritual Practice in Ancient Greece* (Berkeley, CA: University of California Press, 2004). New and important reappraisal of women and cult in ancient Greece.

Dionysus

Bremmer, 'Greek Maenadism Reconsidered'. J. Bremmer, 'Greek Maenadism Reconsidered', *Zeitschrift für Papyrologie und Epigraphik* 55 (1984) pp. 267-86. One of the earlier, somewhat sceptical re-evaluations of Euripides' presentation of Dionysiac cult.

Detienne, *Dionysos at Large*. M. Detienne, *Dionysos at Large*, translated by A. Goldhammer (Cambridge, MA: Harvard University Press, 1989). Structuralist account of Dionysus' place in Greek myth and religion.

Henrichs, 'Greek Maenadism'. A. Henrichs, 'Greek Maenadism from Olympias to Messalina', *Harvard Studies in Classical Philology* 82 (1978), pp. 121-60. Pioneering re-evaluation of Dionysus-cult.

Guide to Further Reading

Henrichs, 'Greek and Roman Glimpses'. A. Henrichs, 'Greek and Roman Glimpses of Dionysos', pp. 1-11 in C. Houser (editor), *Dionysos and his Circle: Ancient through Modern* (Cambridge, MA: Fogg Art Museum, 1979), pp. 1-11. Brief overview of Dionysus in art, religion and literature.

Henrichs, 'He Has a God'. A. Henrichs, '"He Has a God in Him:" Human and Divine in the Modern Perception of Dionysus', in T. Carpenter and C. Faraone (editors), *Masks of Dionysus* (Ithaca, NY: Cornell University Press, 1993), pp. 13-43. Excellent outline of Dionysiac religion.

Henrichs, *OCD*. A. Henrichs, 'Dionysus', in S. Hornblower and A. Spawforth (editors), *Oxford Classical Dictionary*, 3rd edition (Oxford: Oxford University Press, 2003), pp. 479-82. Essential overview of Dionysus in Athenian culture with useful bibliography.

Masks. T.H. Carpenter and C.A. Faraone (editors), *Masks of Dionysus* (Ithaca, NY: Cornell University Press, 1993). Essential collection of articles on Dionysus and the *Bacchae*.

Otto, *Dionysus*. W. Otto, *Dionysus, Myth and Cult*, translated by R. Palmer. Originally published in 1933 (Bloomington, IN: Indiana University Press, 1965). Influenced by Nietzsche and Rohde. The ancestor of mainstream modern criticism of the play.

Versnel, *Ter Unus*. H. Versnel, *Ter Unus: Isis, Dionysus, Hermes: Three Studies in Henotheism* (Leiden: E.J. Brill, 1990). Links play with fifth-century Athenian religion.

Tragedy

Dionysus Since 69. E. Hall, F. Macintosh and A. Wrigley (editors), *Dionysus Since 69: Greek Tragedy at the Dawn of the Third Millennium* (Oxford: Oxford University Press, 2004). Fascinating collection of essays on Greek tragedy in modern performance.

Easterling, 'A Show for Dionysus'. P. Easterling, 'A Show for Dionysus', in P. Easterling (editor), *The Cambridge Companion to Greek Tragedy* (Cambridge: Cambridge University Press, 1997), pp. 36-53. Discussion of Dionysus and tragedy.

Goldhill, *Reading Greek Tragedy*. S. Goldhill, *Reading Greek Tragedy* (Cambridge: Cambridge University Press, 1986). Excellent general treatment of tragedy.

Goldhill, 'The Great Dionysia'. S. Goldhill, 'The Great Dionysia and Civic Ideology', in J. Winkler and F. Zeitlin (editors), *Nothing to do with Dionysos?* (Princeton, NJ: Princeton University Press, 1990), pp. 97-129. On the civic aspects of Greek tragedy.

Pickard-Cambridge, *Dramatic Festivals*. A. Pickard-Cambridge, *The Dramatic Festivals of Athens*, 1st edition Oxford 1953; 2nd edition revised by J. Gould and D. M. Lewis and reissued with new supple-

ment (Oxford: Clarendon Press, 1988). Fundamental work on Greek theatre.
Silk and Stern, *Nietzsche on Tragedy*. M.S. Silk and J.P. Stern, *Nietzsche on Tragedy* (Cambridge: Cambridge University Press, 1981). Very detailed study of the *Birth of Tragedy*.
Sourvinou-Inwood, *Tragedy and Athenian Religion*. C. Sourvinou-Inwood, *Tragedy and Athenian Religion* (Lanham, Boulder, New York, Oxford: Lexington Books, 2003). Discusses the religious and specifically Dionysian origins of Greek tragedy. Her conception of the gods in tragedy is very different from mine and well worth reading.
Taplin, *Greek Tragedy*. O. Taplin, *Greek Tragedy in Action* (London: Methuen, 1978). Emphasises the visual, as well as the textual aspects of tragedy.

General books and articles on Euripides

Conacher, *Euripidean Drama*. D. Conacher, *Euripidean Drama: Myth, Theme and Structure* (Toronto: University of Toronto Press, 1967). Good general introduction.
Grube, *Drama of Euripides*. G.M.A. Grube, *The Drama of Euripides* (New York: Barnes & Noble, 1961). Solid general study.

Treatments of the *Bacchae*

Foley, 'Masque'. H. Foley, 'The Masque of Dionysus', reprinted in J. Mossman (editor), *Oxford Readings in Classical Studies: Euripides* (Oxford: Oxford University Press, 2003), pp. 342-68. Very influential article emphasising the metatheatrical aspects of the play.
Leinieks, *City of Dionysos*. V. Leinieks, *The City of Dionysos: A Study of Euripides' Bacchae* (Stuttgart and Leipzig: Teubner, 1996). A long book containing some interesting insights: hostility to Segal et al. makes it less perhaps useful than it might otherwise be.
Oranje, *Euripides' Bacchae*. H. Oranje *Euripides' Bacchae: The Play and its Audience: Mnemosyne Supplement 78* (Leiden: E.J. Brill, 1984). Detailed, traditionally-oriented survey. Includes a helpful section on fragmentary Dionysus-tragedy.
Seaford, *Reciprocity*. R. Seaford, *Reciprocity and Ritual: Homer and Tragedy in the Developing Greek City State* (Oxford: Clarendon Press, 1994). Important background to Seaford's later work on the *Bacchae*.
Segal, 'Bacchae as Metatragedy'. C. Segal, 'The Bacchae as Metatragedy', in P. Burian (editor), *Directions in Euripidean Criticism* (Durham, NC: Duke University Press, 1985), pp. 156-73. Accessible account of metatragedy in the *Bacchae*.

Segal, 'Language of the Self'. C. Segal, 'Euripides' *Bacchae*: The Language of the Self and the Language of the Mysteries', in C. Segal, *Interpreting Greek Tragedy: Myth, Poetry, Text* (Ithaca, NY: Cornell University Press, 1986), pp. 294-312. On religion, language and psychology in the play.

Segal, 'Pentheus on the Couch'. C. Segal, 'Pentheus and Hippolytus on the Couch and on the Grid: Psychoanalytic and Structuralist Readings of Greek Tragedy', in *Classical World* 72 (1978/9), pp. 129-48, reprinted in C. Segal, *Interpreting Greek Tragedy: Myth, Poetry, Text* (Ithaca, NY: Cornell University Press, 1986), pp. 268-93. Accessible introduction to structuralist and psychological criticism of the play.

Segal, *Dionysiac Poetics*. C. Segal, *Dionysiac Poetics and Euripides' Bacchae Expanded with a New Afterword by the Author* (Princeton, NJ: Princeton University Press, 1997). Fundamental to any consideration of the play.

Segal, 'Lament and Recognition'. C. Segal, 'Lament and Recognition: A Reconsideration of the Ending of the *Bacchae*', *Illinois Classical Studies* 24-5, (1999-2000), pp. 273-91. Clear account of issues concerning the lost portions at the end of the play.

Winnington Ingram, *Euripides and Dionysus*. R.P. Winnington Ingram, *Euripides and Dionysus: An Interpretation of the Bacchae* (Cambridge: Cambridge University Press, 1948). Still a superb treatment of the play: very hostile to Dionysus.

Dionysus and the *Bacchae* after Euripides

Goldhill, 'Modern Critical Approaches'. S. Goldhill, 'Modern Critical Approaches to Tragedy', in P. Easterling (editor), *The Cambridge Companion to Greek Tragedy* (Cambridge: Cambridge University Press, 1997), pp. 324-47. Overview of the main modern critical positions on the *Bacchae*.

Henrichs, 'Loss of Self'. A. Henrichs, 'Loss of Self, Suffering, Violence: The Modern View of Dionysus from Nietzsche to Girard', *Harvard Studies in Classical Philology* 88 (1984), pp. 205-40. Overview of attitudes towards Dionysus from Nietzsche onwards.

Lucas, *Euripides and his Influence*. F.L. Lucas, *Euripides and his Influence* (New York: Cooper Square Publishers, 1963). A useful book on Euripides and later literature.

Bibliography

H.E. Adams et al., 'Is Homophobia Associated With Homosexual Arousal?', *Journal of Abnormal Psychology* 105 (1996), pp. 440-5.

W. Arrowsmith (translator), Euripides' *Bacchae* (Chicago: University of Chicago Press, 1959).

M. Arthur, 'The Choral Odes of the *Bacchae* of Euripides', *Yale Classical Studies* 22 (1972), pp. 145-79.

A. Aviram, 'Postmodern Gay Dionysus: Dr. Frank N. Furter', *Journal of Popular Culture* 26:3 (1992), pp. 183-92.

R. Baker-White, 'The Politics of Ritual in Wole Soyinka's *The Bacchae of Euripides*', *Comparative Drama* 27 (1993), pp. 377-398.

S. Barlow, *The Imagery of Euripides: A Study in the Dramatic Use of Pictorial Language* (London: Methuen, 1971).

J. Barrett, 'Pentheus and the Spectator in Euripides' *Bacchae*', *American Journal of Philology* 119 (1998), pp. 337-60.

E.M. Blaiklock, *The Male Characters of Euripides: A Study in Realism* (Wellington: New Zealand University Press, 1952).

G.W. Bond, *Euripides: Heracles* (Oxford: Clarendon Press, 1988).

R. Bond, '(Re)inventing Euripides' *Bacchae*', in J. Barsby (editor), *Greek and Roman Drama: Translation and Performance* (Stuttgart and Weimar: J.B. Metzler, 2002), pp. 49-57.

J. Bowen, *The Disorderly Women* (London: Methuen, 1969).

J. Bremmer, 'Scapegoat Rituals in Ancient Greece', *Harvard Studies in Classical Philology* 87 (1983), pp. 299-320.

—————— 'Greek Maenadism Revisited', *Zeitschrift für Papyrologie und Epigraphik* 55 (1984), pp. 267-86.

—————— 'Transvestite Dionysos', in M.W. Padilla (editor), *Rites of Passage in Ancient Greece: Literature, Religion, Society* (Lewisburg and London: Bucknell University Press, 1999), pp. 183-200.

P. Brown, 'Greek Tragedy in the Opera House and Concert Hall of the late Twentieth Century', in E. Hall, F. Macintosh and A. Wrigley (editors), *Dionysus Since 69: Greek Tragedy at the Dawn of the Third Millennium* (Oxford: Oxford University Press, 2004), pp. 285-309.

P. Burian, *Directions in Euripidean Criticism* (Durham, NC: Duke University Press, 1985).

—————— 'Tragedy Adapted for Stage and Screens: the Renaissance to the Present', in P. Easterling (editor), *Cambridge Companion to Greek Drama* (Cambridge: Cambridge University Press, 1997), pp. 228-83.

W. Burkert, *Homo Necans: the Anthropology of Ancient Greek Sacrificial Ritual and Myth*, translated by P. Bing (Berkeley, CA: University of California Press, 1983).

—— *Greek Religion*, translated by J. Raffan (Cambridge, MA: Harvard University Press, 1985).

—— *Ancient Mystery Cults* (Cambridge, MA: Harvard University Press, 1987).

A. Burnett, 'Pentheus and Dionysus: Host and Guest', *Classical Philology* 65 (1970), pp.15-29.

R. Buxton, 'The Messenger and the Maenads: A Speech in Euripides' *Bacchae* 1043-1152', *Acta Antiqua Academiae Scientiarum Hungaricae* (*AAHung*) 32 (1989), pp. 225-34.

T. Carpenter, *Dionysian Imagery in Fifth-Century Athens* (Oxford: Oxford University Press, 1986).

T. Carpenter and C. Faraone (editors), *Masks of Dionysus* (Ithaca, NY: Cornell University Press, 1993).

J. Carrière, 'Sur le message des *Bacchantes*', *Antiquité Classique* 35 (1966), pp.118-39.

P. Cartledge, *The Greeks: A Portrait of Self and Others* (Oxford and New York: Oxford University Press, 1993).

V. Castellani, 'That Troubled House of Pentheus in Euripides' *Bacchae*', *Transactions of the American Philological Association* 106 (1976), pp. 61-83.

D. Cohen, 'Seclusion, Separation and the Status of Women', *Greece and Rome* 36 (1989), pp. 3-15.

M. Colakis, *The Classics and the American Theater of the 1960s and Early 1970s* (Lanham, MD: University Press of America, 1993).

C. Collard, *Euripides: Greece and Rome New Surveys in the Classics* 14 (Oxford: Clarendon Press, 1981).

D. Conacher, *Euripidean Drama: Myth, Theme and Structure* (Toronto: University of Toronto Press, 1967).

M. Cropp, 'TI TO SOPHON?', *Bulletin of the Institute of Classical Studies* 28 (1981), pp. 39-42.

E. Csapo and W.J. Slater, *The Context of Ancient Drama* (Ann Arbor: University of Michigan Press, 1995).

S. des Bouvrie, 'Euripides *Bakkhai* and Maenadism', *Classica et Medievalia* 48 (1997), pp.75-114.

M. Detienne, *Dionysos at Large*, translated by A. Goldhammer (Cambridge, MA: Harvard University Press, 1989).

G. Devereux, 'The Psychotherapy Scene in Euripides' *Bacchae*', *Journal of Hellenic Studies* 90 (1970), pp. 35-48.

J. Diggle, *Euripidis Fabulae* III (Oxford: Clarendon Press, 1994).

Bibliography

T. Disch, Review of the *Bacchae*, *The Nation* 12 September 1987, pp. 246-7.

E.R. Dodds, *The Greeks and the Irrational* (Berkeley, CA: University of California Press, 1951).

―――― *Euripides: Bacchae* (Oxford: Oxford University Press, 1960).

―――― 'Euripides the Irrationalist', in E.R. Dodds, *The Ancient Concept of Progress and Other Essays in Greek Literature and Belief* (Oxford: Oxford University Press, 1973), pp. 78-91.

K. Dover, *Aristophanes: Frogs*, (Oxford: Clarendon Press, 1993).

M. Duffy, *Rites*, in V. Sullivan and J. Hatch (editors), *Plays By and About Women* (New York: Random House, 1973), pp. 349-77.

R. Dyer, 'Image and Symbol: The Link Between the Two Worlds of the *Bacchae*', *Journal of the Australasian Universities Language and Literature Association* 21 (1964), pp. 15-26.

P. Easterling, 'Constructing Character in Greek Tragedy', in C. Pelling (editor), *Characterisation and Individuality in Greek Literature* (Oxford: Clarendon Press, 1990), pp. 81-99.

―――― 'A Show for Dionysus', in P. Easterling (editor), *The Cambridge Companion to Greek Tragedy* (Cambridge: Cambridge University Press, 1997), pp. 36-53.

―――― *The Cambridge Companion to Greek Tragedy* (Cambridge: Cambridge University Press, 1997).

R. Edmonds, 'Tearing Apart the Zagreus Myth: A Few Disparaging Remarks on Orphism and Original Sin', *Classical Antiquity* 18 (1999), pp. 35-73.

L. Edmunds, 'The Religiosity of Alexander', *Greek, Roman and Byzantine Studies* 12 (1971), pp. 363-91.

D. Epstein (translator), 'Euripides' *Bacchae*', in D. Slavitt and P. Bovie (editors), *Euripides, 1: Medea, Hecuba, Andromache, the Bacchae* (Philadelphia, PA: University of Pennsylvania Press, 1997).

S. Esposito (translator), Euripides' *Bacchae* (Newburyport, MA: Focus, 1998) and in *Euripides: Medea, Heracles, Hippolytus, Bacchae* (Newburyport, MA, Focus, 2002).

E. Faas, *Tragedy and After: Euripides, Shakespeare, Goethe* (Kingston and Montreal: McGill-Queen's University Press, 1984).

L. Farnell, *Cults of the Greek States* V (Oxford: Clarendon Press, 1909).

A.J. Festugière, 'Euripide dans Les *Bacchantes*', *Eranos* 55 (1957), pp. 127-44.

R. Fisher, 'The "Palace Miracles" in Euripides' *Bacchae*: A Reconsideration', *American Journal of Philology* 113 (1992), pp. 179-88.

H. Foley, 'Twentieth Century Performance and Adaptation of Euripides', *Illinois Classical Studies* 24-5 (1999-2001), pp. 1-13.

―――― 'The Masque of Dionysus', reprinted in J. Mossman (editor),

Oxford Readings in Classical Studies: Euripides (Oxford: Oxford University Press, 2003), pp. 342-68.

—— 'Bad Women: Gender Politics in Late 20th Century Performance and Revision of Greek Tragedy', in E. Hall, F. Macintosh and A. Wrigley (editors), *Dionysus Since 69: Greek Tragedy at the Dawn of the Third Millennium* (Oxford: Oxford University Press, 2004), pp. 77-111.

S. Freud, *Totem and Taboo*, translated by J. Strachey (New York: Norton, 1950).

R. Friedrich, 'Dionysus Among the Dons: The New Ritualism in Richard Seaford's Commentary on the *Bacchae*', *Arion* 7 (2000), pp. 115-52.

B. Friel, *Wonderful Tennessee* (Oldcastle: Gallery Press, 1993).

R. Gibbons, *Euripides' Bakkhai with Introduction and Notes by Charles Segal* (New York: Oxford University Press, 2001).

R. Girard, *Violence and the Sacred*, translated by P. Gregory (Baltimore, MD: Johns Hopkins University Press, 1977).

B. Goff, *Citizen Bacchae: Women's Ritual Practice in Ancient Greece* (Berkeley, CA: University of California Press, 2004).

S. Goldhill, *Reading Greek Tragedy* (Cambridge: Cambridge University Press, 1986).

—— 'Doubling and Recognition in the *Bacchae*', *Metis* 3 (1988), pp. 137-55.

—— 'The Great Dionysia and Civic Ideology', in J. Winkler and F. Zeitlin (editors), *Nothing to do with Dionysus?* (Princeton, NJ: Princeton University Press, 1990), pp. 97-129.

—— 'Representing Democracy: Women at the Great Dionysia', in *Ritual, Finance, Politics: Democratic Accounts Presented to David Lewis* (Oxford: Clarendon Press, 1994), pp. 347-69.

—— 'Modern Critical Approaches to Tragedy', in P. Easterling (editor), *The Cambridge Companion to Greek Tragedy* (Cambridge: Cambridge, 1997), pp. 324-47.

—— 'Civic Ideology and the Problem of Difference: The Politics of Aeschylean Tragedy Once Again', *Journal of Hellenic Studies* 120 (2000), pp. 34-56.

J. Gould, 'Dramatic Character and "Human Intelligibility" in Greek Tragedy', *Proceedings of the Cambridge Philological Society* 33 (1978), pp. 43-67.

F. Graf, 'Dionysian And Orphic Eschatology: New Texts and Old Questions', in T. Carpenter and C. Faraone (editors), *Masks of Dionysus* (Ithaca, NY: Cornell University Press, 1993), pp. 239-58.

L. Greenwood, *Aspects of Euripidean Tragedy* (New York: Russell and Russell, 1952).

J. Gregory, 'Some Aspects of Seeing in Euripides' *Bacchae*', *Greece and Rome* 32 (1985), pp. 23-31.

Bibliography

J. Griffin, 'The Social Function of Attic Tragedy,' *Classical Quarterly* 48 (1998), pp. 39-61.

G. Grube, *The Drama of Euripides* (New York: Barnes and Noble, 1961; originally London, 1941).

W. Guthrie, *The Greeks and Their Gods* (Boston, MA: Beacon Press, 1950).

E. Hall, *Inventing the Barbarian* (Oxford: Oxford University Press, 1989).

—— 'The Sociology of Athenian Tragedy', in P. Easterling (editor), *The Cambridge Companion to Greek Tragedy* (Cambridge: Cambridge University Press, 1997), pp. 93-127.

—— 'Introduction', in E. Hall, F. Macintosh and A. Wrigley (editors), *Dionysus Since 69: Greek Tragedy at the Dawn of the Third Millennium* (Oxford: Oxford University Press, 2004).

L. Hardwick, 'The Play's the Thing: Modern Staging of the *Bacchae*', *Dionysus* 15 (2001), pp. 24-9.

K. Hartigan, *Greek Tragedy on the American Stage: Ancient Drama in the Commercial Theatre 1882-1994* (Westport, CT: Greenwood Press, 1995).

J. Henderson, 'Women and the Athenian Dramatic Festivals', *Transactions of the American Philological Society* 121 (1991), pp. 133-47.

A. Henrichs, 'Greek Maenadism from Olympias to Messalina', *Harvard Studies in Classical Philology* 82 (1978), pp. 121-60.

—— 'Greek and Roman Glimpses of Dionysos', in C. Houser, *Dionysos and his Circle: Ancient through Modern* (Cambridge, MA: Fogg Art Museum, 1979), pp. 1-11.

—— 'Loss of Self, Suffering, Violence: The Modern View of Dionysus from Nietzsche to Girard', *Harvard Studies in Classical Philology* 88 (1984), pp. 205-40.

—— 'Male Intruders among the Maenads: the So-called Male Celebrant', in H. Evjen (editor), *Mnemai: Classical Studies in Memory of Karl K. Hulley* (Chico, CA: Scholars Press, 1984), pp. 69-91.

—— '"He Has a God in Him": Human and Divine in the Modern Perception of Dionysus', in T. Carpenter and C. Faraone (editors), *Masks of Dionysus* (Ithaca, NY: Cornell University Press, 1993), pp. 13-43.

—— 'Dionysus', *Oxford Classical Dictionary*, 3rd edition, S. Hornblower and A. Spawforth (editors) (Oxford: Oxford University Press, 2003), pp. 479-82.

C. Houser, 'Changing Views of Dionysos', in C. Houser, *Dionysos and his Circle: Ancient through Modern* (Cambridge, MA: Fogg Art Museum, 1979), pp. 12-24.

E. Howald, *Die Griechische Tragödie* (Munich: Oldenbourg, 1930).

Bibliography

M. Jameson, 'The Asexuality of Dionysus', in T. Carpenter and C. Faraone (editors), *Masks of Dionysus* (Ithaca, NY: Cornell University Press, 1993), pp. 44-64.

E. Jones, *Wole Soyinka* (New York: Twayne Publishers, 1973).

R. Just, *Women in Athenian Law and Life* (London: Routledge, 1989).

G.S. Kirk, *The Bacchae. A Translation with Commentary* (Englewood Cliffs, NJ: Prentice-Hall, 1970 and Cambridge University Press, 1970).

A. Kirkhoff, 'Ein Supplement zu Euripides *Bacchae*', *Philologus* 8 (1853), pp. 78-94.

B. Knox, 'Euripides: The Poet as Prophet', in P. Burian, *Directions in Euripidean Criticism* (Durham, NC: Duke University Press, 1985), pp. 1-12.

J. Kott, *The Eating of the Gods* (New York: Random House, 1970).

D. Kovacs, *The Heroic Muse: Studies in the Hippolytus and Hecuba of Euripides* (Baltimore, MD: Johns Hopkins University Press, 1987), pp. 1-21.

———*Bacchae; Iphigenia at Aulis; Rhesus* (Cambridge, MA: Harvard University Press, 2002).

D. Lan and C. Churchill, *A Mouthful of Birds* (London: Methuen, 1986).

M. Lefkowitz, *Lives of the Greek Poets* (Baltimore, MD: Johns Hopkins University Press, 1981).

——— '"Impiety" and "Atheism" in Euripides' Dramas', *Classical Quarterly* 39 (1989), pp. 70-82.

V. Leinieks, *The City of Dionysos: A Study of Euripides' Bacchae* (Stuttgart and Leipzig: Teubner, 1996).

B. Lewis, Review of the *Bacchae*, *The Stage*, 13th November 2003.

H. Lloyd-Jones, Appendix to *Aeschylus*, H.W. Smyth translation (Cambridge, MA: Harvard University Press, 1963).

F. Lucas, *Euripides and his Influence* (New York: Cooper Square Publishers, 1963).

F. Macintosh, 'Tragedy in Performance: Nineteenth and Twentieth Century Productions', in P. Easterling (editor), *The Cambridge Companion to Greek Tragedy* (Cambridge: Cambridge University Press, 1997), pp. 284-323.

D. Mahon, *The Bacchae: After Euripides* (Oldcastle: Gallery Press, 1991).

J. March, 'Euripides' *Bakchai*: A Reconstruction in the Light of Vase Painting', *Bulletin of the Institute of Classical Studies* 36 (1989), pp. 33-65.

M. McDonald, 'L'extase de Penthée: ivresse et représentation dans les *Bacchantes* d'Euripide', *Pallas* 38 (1992), pp. 227-37.

——— *Ancient Sun, Modern Light: Greek Drama on the Modern Stage* (New York: Columbia University Press, 1992).

Bibliography

——— 'Moving Icons: Teaching Euripides in Film', in R. Mitchell-Boyask (editor), *Approaches to Teaching the Dramas of Euripides* (New York, Modern Language Association of America, 2002), pp. 60-6.

P. McGinty, *Interpretation and Dionysus: Method in the Study of a God* (The Hague: Mouton, 1978).

H. Merklin, *Gott und Mensch im 'Hippolytos' und den 'Bakchen' des Euripides* (Freiburg: J. Krause, 1964).

A. Michelini, *Euripides and the Tragic Tradition* (Wisconsin: University of Wisconsin Press, 1987).

J. Mikalson, *Honor Thy Gods: Popular Religion in Greek Tragedy* (Chapel Hill, NC: University of North Carolina Press, 1991).

R. Milgate, *A Refined Look at Existence* (London: Methuen, 1968).

R. Mitchell-Boyask (editor), *Approaches to Teaching the Dramas of Euripides* (New York: Modern Language Association of Euripides, 2002).

J. Morwood, *Iphigenia among the Taurians, Bacchae, Iphigenia at Aulis, Rhesus with an Introduction and Select Bibliography by Edith Hall* (Oxford: Oxford University Press, 1999).

G. Murray, Appendix to Jane Harrison, *Themis: A Study in the Social Origins of Greek Religion* (Cambridge: Cambridge University Press, 1912).

——— *Euripides Fabulae* III (Oxford: Clarendon Press, 1913).

——— *Euripides and his Age*, 2nd edition (London: Oxford University Press, 1946).

J. Neils and J. Oakley, *Coming of Age in Classical Athens: Images of Childhood from the Classical Past* (New Haven and London: Yale University Press, 2003).

F. Nietzsche, *The Birth of Tragedy* (Leipzig: E.W. Fritzsch, 1872).

G. Norwood, *The Riddle of the Bacchae* (Manchester: Manchester University Press, 1908).

——— *Essays on Euripidean Drama* (Berkeley, CA: University of California Press, 1954).

A. Nouryeh, 'Soyinka's Euripides: Postcolonial Resistance or Avant-garde Adaptation?', *Research in African Literatures* 34 (2001) pp. 160-71.

D. Obbink, 'Dionysos Poured Out: Ancient and Modern Theories of Sacrifice and Cultural Formation', T. Carpenter and C. Faraone (editors), *Masks of Dionysus* (Ithaca, NY: Cornell University Press, 1993), pp. 65-86.

H. Oranje, *Euripides' Bacchae: The Play and its Audience: Mnemosyne Supplement 78* (Leiden: E.J. Brill, 1984).

M. Orban, 'Les *Bacchantes*: Euripide fidèle a lui-meme', *Les Etudes Classiques* 52 (1984), pp. 217-32.

W. Otto, *Dionysus, Myth and Cult*, translated by R. Palmer. Originally published in 1933 (Bloomington, IN: Indiana University Press, 1965).

R. Padel, 'Women: Model for Possession by Greek Daemons', in A. Cameron and A. Kuhrt (editors), *Images of Women in Antiquity* (Detroit: Wayne State Press, 1983), pp. 3-19.

H. Parke, *Festivals of the Athenians* (Ithaca, NY: Cornell University Press, 1977).

R. Parker, 'Gods Cruel and Kind: Tragic and Civic Theology', in C. Pelling (editor), *Greek Tragedy and the Historian* (Oxford: Clarendon Press, 1997), pp. 143-60.

H. Partch, *Genesis of a Music: An Account of a Creative Work, its Roots and its Fulfillments*, 2nd edition (New York: Da Capo Press, 1979).

S. Philippo, Review of Seaford's *Commentary*, *Classical Review* 47 (1997), pp. 252-3.

A. Pickard-Cambridge, *The Dramatic Festivals of Athens*, 2nd edition revised by J. Gould and D. Lewis and reissued with new supplement (Oxford: Clarendon Press, 1988).

A. Podlecki, 'Individual and Group in Euripides' *Bacchae*', *Antiquité Classique* 43 (1974), pp. 143-65.

J.I. Porter, *The Invention of Dionysus: An Essay on The Birth of Tragedy* (Stanford, CA: Stanford University Press, 2000).

R. Rehm, *Greek Tragic Theatre* (London: Routledge, 1992).

D. Roberts, 'Parting Words: Final Lines in Sophocles and Euripides', *Classical Quarterly* 37 (1987), pp. 51-64.

———— 'Euripides in Translation', in R. Mitchell-Boyask (editor), *Approaches to Teaching the Dramas of Euripides* (New York: Modern Language Association of America, 2002), pp. 38-50.

P. Roche, *Three Plays of Euripides: Alcestis, Medea, The Bacchae* (New York: Norton, 1974).

E. Rohde, *Psyche*, originally published in 1894 and translated by W.B. Hillis (London: K. Paul, Trench, Trubner, 1925).

J. de Romilly, 'Le thème du bonheur dans les *Bacchantes*', *Revue des Etudes Grecques* 76 (1963), pp. 361-80.

D. Rosenbloom, 'Shouting "Fire" in a Crowded Theatre: Phrynichus' *Capture of Miletos* and the Politics of Fear in Early Attic Tragedy', *Philologus* 137 (1993), pp. 159-96.

P. Roth, 'Teiresias as Mantis and Intellectual in Euripides' *Bacchae*', *Transactions of the American Philological Society* 114 (1984), pp. 59-69.

W. Sale, 'The Psychoanalysis of Pentheus in the Bacchae of Euripides', *Yale Classical Studies* 22 (1972), pp. 63-82.

———— *Existentialism and Euripides: Sickness, Tragedy and Divinity in the Medea, the Hippolytus and the Bacchae* (Berwick: Aureal, 1977).

J. Sandys, *Euripides' Bacchae* (Cambridge: Cambridge University Press, 1900).

Bibliography

R. Seaford, 'Dionysiac Drama and the Dionysiac Mysteries', *Classical Quarterly* 31 (1981), pp. 252-75.

—— 'Dionysus as Destroyer of the Household: Homer, Tragedy and the Polis', in T. Carpenter and C. Faraone (editors), *Masks of Dionysus* (Ithaca, NY: Cornell University Press, 1993), pp. 115-46.

—— *Reciprocity and Ritual: Homer and Tragedy in the Developing City State* (Oxford: Clarendon Press, 1994).

—— *Euripides: Bacchae* (Warminster: Aris and Phillips, 1996).

—— 'Thunder, Lightning and Earthquake in the *Bacchae* and the *Acts of the Apostles*', in A.B. Lloyd (editor), *What is a God? Studies in the Nature of Greek Divinity* (London: Duckworth, 1997), pp. 139-51.

—— 'Dionysia', in S. Hornblower and A. Spawforth (editors), *Oxford Classical Dictionary*, 3rd edition (Oxford: Oxford University Press, 2003), p. 476.

R. Schechner, 'Radicalism, Sexuality and Performance', *Drama Review* 13 (1968), pp. 89-110.

—— *Dionysus in 69* (New York: Farrar, Strauss and Giroux, 1970).

W. Scott, 'Two Suns Over Thebes: Imagery and Stage Effects in the *Bacchae*', *Transactions of the American Philological* Association 105 (1975), pp. 333-46.

C. Segal, 'Euripides' *Bacchae*: Conflict and Mediation', *Ramus* 6 (1977), pp. 103-20.

—— 'Etymologies and Double meanings in Euripides' *Bacchae*', *Glotta* 60 (1982), pp. 81-93.

—— 'The Bacchae as Metatragedy', in P. Burian (editor), *Directions in Euripidean Criticism* (Durham, NC: Duke University Press, 1985), pp. 156-73.

—— 'Pentheus and Hippolytus on the Couch and on the Grid: Psychoanalytic and Structuralist Readings of Greek Tragedy', *Classical World* 72 (1978/9) pp. 129-48 reprinted in *Interpreting Greek Tragedy: Myth, Poetry, Text* (Ithaca, NY: Cornell University Press, 1986), pp. 268-93.

—— 'Euripides' *Bacchae*: The Language of the Self and the Language of the Mysteries', in *Interpreting Greek Tragedy: Myth, Poetry, Text* (Ithaca, NY: Cornell University Press, 1986), pp. 294-312.

—— *Interpreting Greek Tragedy: Myth, Poetry, Text* (Ithaca, NY: Cornell University Press, 1986).

—— 'Chorus and Community in Euripides' *Bacchae*', in L. Edmunds and R. Wallace (editors), *Poet, Public and Performance: Ancient Genres* (Baltimore, MD: Johns Hopkins University Press, 1997), pp. 65-86.

—— *Dionysiac Poetics and Euripides' Bacchae Expanded with a New Afterword by the Author* (Princeton, NJ: Princeton University Press, 1997).

Bibliography

—— 'Lament and Recognition: A Reconsideration of the Ending of the *Bacchae*', *Illinois Classical Studies* 24-5 (1999-2000), pp. 273-91.

B. Seidensticker, 'Pentheus', *Poetica* 6 (1972), pp. 35-63.

—— 'Comic Elements in Euripides' *Bacchae*', *American Journal of Philology* 99 (1978), pp. 303-20.

B. Seidensticker, 'Sacrificial Ritual in the *Bacchae*', in *Arktouros: Hellenic Studies Presented to Bernard M.W. Knox* (Berlin: de Gruyter, 1979), pp. 181-90.

M.S. Silk and J.P. Stern, *Nietzsche on Tragedy* (Cambridge: Cambridge University Press, 1981).

J.Z. Smith, 'The Devil in Mr Jones', in *Imagining Religion from Babylon to Jonestown* (Chicago: University of Chicago Press, 1982), pp. 102-20.

C. Sourvinou-Inwood, 'Tragedy and Religion: Constructs and Readings', in C. Pelling (editor), *Greek Tragedy and the Historian* (Oxford: Clarendon Press, 1997), pp. 161-86.

—— *Tragedy and Athenian Religion* (Lanham, Boulder, New York, Oxford: Lexington Books, 2003).

W. Soyinka, *The Bacchae of Euripides: A Communion Rite* (London: Eyre Methuen, 1973).

P.T. Stevens, 'Euripides and the Athenians', *Journal of Hellenic Studies* 76 (1956), pp. 87-94.

O. Taplin, *Greek Tragedy in Action* (London: Methuen, 1978).

D. Tartt, *The Secret History* (New York: Knopff, 1992).

C. Teevan, *Bacchai: Euripides: A New Translation* (London: Oberon, 2002).

P. Vellacott, *The Bacchae and Other Plays* (Harmondsworth, Penguin: 1954).

J.P. Vernant, 'Dionysus', in Mircea Eliade et al. (editors), *The Encyclopedia of Religion* (New York: MacMillan, 1987), pp. 113-4.

—— 'The Masked Dionysus', in J.P. Vernant, *Myth and Tragedy in Ancient Greece* (New York: Zone, 1988), pp. 381-412.

—— *Myth and Tragedy in Ancient Greece* (New York: Zone, 1988).

A.W. Verrall, *Euripides, the Rationalist: A Study in the History of Arts and Religion,* (Cambridge: Cambridge University Press, 1895).

—— *The Bacchae of Euripides and Other Essays* (Cambridge: Cambridge University Press, 1910).

H. Versnel, *Ter Unus: Isis, Dionysus, Hermes: Three Studies in Henotheism* (Leiden: E.J. Brill, 1990).

C. Voinovich, Review of Paul Woodruff (translation), *Euripides: Bacchae, Bryn Mawr Classical Review* 2001-01-04.

J.M. Walton, *Greek Theatre Practice* (Westport, CT: Greenwood Press, 1980).

Bibliography

————— *Living Greek Theatre: A Handbook of Classical Performance and Modern Production* (New York, Westport, CT and London: Greenwood Press, 1987).

————— *Euripides: Plays I: Medea, The Phoenician Women, Bacchae* (London: Methuen, 1998).

T.B.L. Webster, *The Tragedies of Euripides* (London: Methuen, 1967).

M. West, 'Tragica VII', *Bulletin of the Institute of Classical Studies* 39 (1983), pp. 63-82.

D. White, *Wole Soyinka Revisited* (New York: Twayne, 1993).

D. Wiles, *Tragedy in Athens: Performance Space and Theatrical Meaning* (Cambridge: Cambridge University Press, 1997).

————— *Greek Theatre Performance: An Introduction* (Cambridge: Cambridge University Press, 2000).

————— 'The Use of Masks in Modern Performances of Greek Drama', in E. Hall, F. Macintosh and A. Wrigley (editors), *Dionysus Since 69: Greek Tragedy at the Dawn of the Third Millennium* (Oxford: Oxford University Press, 2004), pp. 245-63.

C.K. Williams, *The Bacchae of Euripides* (New York: Noonday Press, 1990).

C.W. Willink, 'Some Problems in the *Bacchae*', *Classical Quarterly* 16 (1966), pp. 27-50, 220-42.

P. Wilson, *The Athenian Institution of the Khoregia: The Chorus, the City and the Stage* (Cambridge: Cambridge University Press, 2000).

J. Winkler and F. Zeitlin (editors) *Nothing to do with Dionysos?: Athenian Drama in its Social Context* (Princeton, NJ: Princeton University Press, 1990).

R.P. Winnington Ingram, *Euripides and Dionysus: An Interpretation of the Bacchae* (Cambridge: Cambridge University Press, 1948).

————— 'Euripides, Poietes Sophos', reprinted in J. Mossman (editor), *Oxford Readings in Classical Studies: Euripides* (Oxford: Oxford University Press, 2003), pp. 47-63.

V. Wohl, Review of V. Leinieks, *The City of Dionysos: A Study of Euripides' Bacchae, Classical Review* 49 (1999).

P. Woodruff, *Euripides: Bacchae* (Hackett: Indianapolis, IN, 1998).

F. Zeitlin, 'Cultic Models of the Female: Rites of Dionysus and Demeter', *Arethusa* 15 (1982), pp. 129-57.

————— 'Thebes: Theatre of Self and Society in Athenian Drama', in J. Winkler and F. Zeitlin (editors), *Nothing to do with Dionysos?: Athenian Drama in its Social Context* (Princeton, NJ: Princeton University Press, 1990), pp. 130-67.

————— 'Staging Dionysus between Thebes and Athens', in *Masks of Dionysus*, C. Faraone and T. Carpenter (Ithaca, NY: Cornell University Press, 1993), pp. 147-82.

————— 'Dionysus in 69', in E. Hall, F. Macintosh and A. Wrigley (editors), *Dionysus Since 69: Greek Tragedy at the Dawn of the*

Third Millennium (Oxford: Oxford University Press, 2004), pp. 49-76.

W. Zürcher, *Die Darstellung des Menschen im Drama des Euripides* (Basel: Reinhardt, 1947).

Chronology

The following is a selection of performances, adaptations and critical work on the *Bacchae*. For a fuller list, see A. Wrigley, 'Details of Productions Discussed' in E. Hall, F. Macintosh and A. Wrigley (editors), *Dionysus Since 69: Greek Tragedy at the Dawn of the Third Millennium* (Oxford: Oxford University Press, 2004), pp. 369-418. Most, but not all, of the productions listed here are mentioned in my text.

405 BCE: Euripides' *Bacchae*.
3rd-2nd cent. BCE: *Pentheus* of Pacuvius (adaptation).
2nd cent. BCE: *Bacchae* of Accius (adaptation).
5th cent. CE: *Dionysiaka* of Nonnus, books 44-6.
1871: F. Nietzsche, *The Birth of Tragedy* (philosophical work on Dionysus).
1908: G. Murray's translation of the *Bacchae*.
1921: Production at London University.
1926: K. Szymanowski, *Krol Roger* (opera).
1930: Production at Cambridge University.
1931: E. Wellesz, *Die Bakchantinnen* (opera).
1934: Production at Smith College.
1935: Production at Bryn Mawr College.
1948: G.F. Ghedini, *Le Bacchanti* (opera).
1960: Second, expanded edition of the *Commentary* on *Bacchae* by E.R. Dodds (first edition originally published in 1943).
1961: H. Partch, *Revelation in the Courthouse Park* (opera).
1964: Production at the Mermaid Theatre, London, with translation by Kenneth Cavander.
1966: H.W. Henze, *The Bassarids*, with libretto by W.H. Auden and C. Kallmann (opera).
1968: R. Schechner, *Dionysus in 69* (adaptation with film in 1970 by Brian de Palma).
1968: R. Milgate, *A Refined Look at Existence* (play).
1968: P. Pasolini, *Teorema* (film).
1969: M. Duffy, *Rites* (play).
1969: J. Bowen, *The Disorderly Women* (play).

Chronology

1973: W. Soyinka, *The Bacchae: A Communion Rite* (play).
1980: Production by M. Cacoyannis at Circle in the Square, New York City.
1981: Production by T. Suzuki, Japan and United States.
1982: R. Travis, *The Black Bacchants* (opera), New York City.
1986: C. Churchill and D. Lan, *A Mouthful of Birds* (play).
1987: Production at the Guthrie Theatre, Minneapolis.
1991: D. Boertz, *Backanterna* (opera directed by Ingmar Bergman), Stockholm.
1992: J. Buller, *Bakxai* (opera), London.
1992: Production in Yaounde, Cameroon.
1992: D. Tartt, *The Secret History* (novel).
1993: Charles Mee, *The Bacchae 2.1* (adaptation).
1993: Brian Friel, *Wonderful Tennessee* (play).
1996: *Dionysus in 96*: a revival of R. Schechner's *Dionysus in 69*, Hawaii.
1996: Operatic adaptation by Beijing Children's Theatre.
1997: C. Segal, *Dionysiac Poetics* (2nd edition.)
1997: Madlab, *Bakkee* (adaption), Columbus, Ohio.
1997: *Trance Bacchae* (multimedia adaptation), Italy.
1997: Production with Paul Schmidt's translation, American Repertory Theatre, Boston (http://www.bostonphoenix.com/archive/theater/97/12/04/THE_BACCHAE.html).
1997: R. Bond, *Dionysus/Diotekk* (adaptation) Christ Church, New Zealand.
1998: Multimedia adaptation by the Performance Technology Research Laboratory, Georgia Institute of Technology.
1999: Oberon Theatre Ensemble, *Bacchae Y2K*, New York City.
2000: Blunt Theatre Company, production directed by S. Morgan, New York City.
2000: Production by the Actors of Dionysus, York.
2001: Production of the *Bacchae* in Malaysia.
2002: Production by Sir Peter Hall, London.
2002: E. Geist, *Die Heimkehr des Dionysus* (musical drama), Vilnius, Lithuania.
2003: Production by the Thiasos Theatre Company, London.
2003: A. Rissik, *Dionysus* (radio play).

Glossary

Antilabe. The division of one line of iambic trimeter between more than one speaker.

Bacchus/Bacchius. Very common cult title of Dionysus, possibly Lydian. The close association between the god and his worshippers is indicated by their name of Bacchi or Bacchae.

Bromius. One of Dionysus' many (cf. Plutarch *Moralia* 388e) titles. Derived from the Greek word *bremô*, 'I roar'. Dionysus is a roaring god in his incarnations as bull and lion and his associations with earthquakes and thunder. An instrument called a bull-roarer was also used in his cult.

Chorêgos. Wealthy private citizen who paid for the training of a tragic chorus.

Dithyramb. Form of choral lyric poem originally sung to, and about, Dionysus. The Great Dionysia at Athens included dithyrambic competitions. Dionysus is called Dithyrambos at *Bacchae* 526: Dodds, *Commentary*, p. 143.

Dochmiacs. Tragic metre restricted to moments of high emotion. ∪– – ∪– is the basic dochmiac rhythm, but many variations are possible.

Eisodoi **or** *parodoi*. Two paths on either side of the stage used as roads to and from the city in which the drama was set.

Episode. Scene of a tragedy.

Euius. Another cult title of Dionysus: 'the god of the cultic cry "euoi"' (good to him).

Exodos. The final scene in a tragedy following the last choral song.

Iacchus. Cult title of Dionysus. Iacchus was an independent god of the Eleusinian procession who became identified with Dionysus.

Iambic trimeter. Metre used for speeches and dialogue. Each line is composed of three 'feet' consisting of two iambs, a metrical unit consisting of one short syllable followed by a long one. The first syllable of each foot can be long or short and variations within the line are possible, but the basic rhythmic pattern is x– ∪– | x– ∪– | x– ∪–.

Maenad. Female ecstatic worshipper of Dionysus. The name is connected with Greek words for madness. Maenads are typically imagined with loose hair, ivy crowns, fawnskin costumes (for warmth and to give them the speed and grace of fawns) and carrying a thyrsus (see below). Drums and flutes accompany them.

170

Metatheatre. Drama which lays emphasis on its own theatrical elements.

Ômophagia. Literally 'raw-eating'. The act of consuming the animal killed by the Maenads in the *sparagmos*.

Orchêstra. 'Dancing place'. Part of the stage where the chorus performed.

Paedagogus. Literally the slave who led the boy from his home to school and back; often also translated as tutor.

Parodos. Song sung by the chorus at their first entry early in the play.

Skênê. Building on the stage which stood for any place entered by the characters in a tragedy.

Sparagmos. The act of tearing into pieces the animal caught at the climax of the hunt of the Maenads (cf. *ômophagia*).

Stasimon. Choral song separating the different scenes (episodes) of the tragedy from one another.

Stichomythia. A stylised conversation between actors speaking to one another in alternating lines. Often used to provide excitement in a tragedy by speeding up its dialogue.

Theologeion. Flat roof of the *skênê*, on which divine epiphanies could take place.

Theoxeny. The welcoming of a disguised god by a human being.

Thiasos. The band of Maenads who carry out Dionysus' rituals.

Thyrsus. Fennel stick with a bunch of ivy leaves tied on the end. One of the typical instruments of Bacchic worship and frequently seen in pictures of Maenads. It was in origin a branch of the god's holy tree and, like the evergreen ivy which is also the god's plant, represents the god's vigour and fertility.

Index

Index

Friel, Brian, 146n148

Hesiod, 23
Homer, 23, 24, 35, 63, 89, 103
Homeric Hymn, 23-5
hunting, 74, 132n9, 133n27,
    135n51

Icarius, *see* Erigone

Lan, David and Caryl Churchill,
    118
language and word-play, 39, 40,
    45, 54, 64-7, 71, 75-6
liberation, 24, 53-4, 123n23,
    132n10, 133n27
lions, 23, 46-7, 68, 134n35
Lycurgus, 23, 24, 35

Maenads, 27-9, 35, 46, 52, 57, 60,
    62-3, 66-7, 74, 76, 101, 103,
    106, 125n8, 127n32, 129n58,
    132n9, 133n17, 170
Macedonia, 8, 83, 132n12
masks, 77, 101, 103, 131n8,
    135nn54-5; *see also* costume,
    metatheatre
Mee, Charles, 108-9
Menander, 103
metatheatre, 76-7, 100-2, 107,
    117, 135nn54-5, 151, 171
metre, 19, 125, 170
Milgate, Rodney, 114
myth and ritual, 21-2, 27-8, 90-6,
    127n29

Nietzsche, Friedrich, 81-3, 121n2
Nonnus, 104

ômophagia, *see sparagmos*
operatic versions of *Bacchae*,
    113-14, 118

Pasolini, Pier Paolo, 118
Pegasus, *see* Erigone

Pentheus
    death of, 67-9
    fails to understand Dionysus,
        41-8, 54, 59-60, 65, 71-2
    justifications for, 61-2, 84-5
    sexuality and, 39, 60-1, 74, 98-
        100, 106-8, 110
    as tyrant, 58-9, 110-11
    women and, 44-5, 85
    Persia and the East, 7, 12-13, 69,
        96; *see also* Dionysus and the
        East
Phrynichus, 9-10, 121
Plato, 16, 124n32
Plutarch, 104
politics, 58, 133nn19-20, 29, 95,
    96-7, 111
psychological realism, 10, 47, 60-
    1, 65-6, 134n37, 98-100

reversal, 11, 64-6, 73, 91-2
Roman literature, 35, 104

sacrifice, 92-4, 134nn32, 34
Schechner, Richard, *see Dionysus
    in 69*
Socrates, 82, 96
Sophocles, 8-10, 34, 59, 80, 99,
    103
sophon/sophia, 38, 40, 41, 43, 45,
    69-72, 131n6
sôphrosynê, 46, 71-2
Soyinka, Wole, 109-11
sparagmos, 21, 27-9, 38, 53, 56-7,
    67-8, 74, 127n31, 171
structuralism, 91-4
Suzuki, Tadashi, 112-13
symbolism, 78-9, 87-90, 96-7,
    105, 139n42, 143n83
    in Greek religion, 88-90, 97-
        100, 108-9

Tartt, Donna, 119, 146n26
textual problems, 47-9, 73, 104,
    131n14